You and Your Child

BIBLE STUDY GUIDE

From the Bible-teaching ministry of

Charles R. Swindoll

INSIGHT FOR LIVING

Charles R. Swindoll is a graduate of Dallas Theological Seminary and has served as senior pastor of the First Evangelical Free Church of Fullerton, California, since 1971. Chuck's radio program, "Insight for Living," began in 1979. In addition to his church and radio ministries, Chuck enjoys writing. He has authored numerous books and booklets on a variety of subjects.

Based on the outlines and transcripts of Chuck's sermons, the study guide text is co-authored by Lee Hough, a graduate of the University of Texas at Arlington and Dallas Theological Seminary. He also wrote the Living Insights sections.

Editor in Chief:
Cynthia Swindoll

Coauthor of Text:
Lee Hough

Assistant Editor:
Wendy Peterson

Copy Editors:
Deborah Gibbs
Cheryl Gilmore
Glenda Schlahta

Designer:
Gary Lett

Publishing System Specialist:
Bob Haskins

Director, Communications Division:
Deedee Snyder

Manager, Creative Services:
Alene Cooper

Project Supervisor:
Susan Nelson

Print Production Manager:
John Norton

Printer:
Sinclair Printing Company

Unless otherwise identified, all Scripture references are from the New American Standard Bible, © The Lockman Foundation 1960, 1962, 1963, 1968, 1971, 1972, 1973, 1975, 1977. Used by permission. Other translations cited are the Amplified Bible [AMPLIFIED] and The Living Bible [LB].

An effort has been made to locate sources and obtain permission where necessary for the quotations used in this book. In the event of any unintentional omission, a modification will gladly be incorporated in future printings.

ISBN 0-8499-8442-4
Printed in the United States of America.

COVER DESIGN: Nina Paris
COVER PHOTOGRAPH: Comstock

CONTENTS

This study guide was written to correspond with the audiocassette series *You and Your Child*. The book *You and Your Child* (Nashville, Tenn.: Thomas Nelson Publishers, 1977) was written several years after the original series was presented to our church in Fullerton, at which time Chuck considerably altered the material to be more appropriate for a reading audience. Since the book would be excellent supplemental reading for your study through this series and to avoid some confusion, the following notes indicate how the guide and cassette series correspond to the chapters in the book.

1. "Knowing Your Child" corresponds to chapter 1, "Mom and Dad . . . Meet Your Child," and the first half of chapter 2, "The Bents in Your Baby," in the book.

2. "Breaking Granddad's Bent" corresponds to the second half of chapter 2 in the book, "The Bents in Your Baby."

3. "Loving Your Child" corresponds with chapter 3 in the book, "You Can't Have One without the Other." This book chapter does not correspond with our guide lesson and tape titled "You Can't Have One without the Other." This sermon in the cassette series represents some additional material not presented in the book.

4. "Shaping the Will with Wisdom" partially corresponds to chapter 6 in the book, "Dealing with Rebellion and Disobedience."

5. "Training Your Child" corresponds with chapter 4 in the book, "Straight Talk on Survival Training."

6. "The Home Training of Jesus" corresponds with chapter 5 in the book with the same title.

7. Both lessons for "You and Your Daughter" correspond with chapter 8 in the book with the same title.

8. "You and Your Son" corresponds with chapter 7 in the book with the same title.

9. "Releasing Your Child" corresponds with chapter 10 in the book with the same title.

The following sermons in the cassette series are not represented in the book: "You Can't Have One without the Other," "The Ministry of the Rod," "Seeds a Mother Plants," and "Masculine Model of Leadership."

Two chapters from the book—chapter 9, "Those Extra-Special Children," and chapter 11, "Hope for the Hurting"—are not included in the cassette series and study guide. We recommend these chapters for those who are experiencing hurt in their family relationships, or for those who desire a few insights about extra-special little ones—children who are adopted, handicapped, unplanned, gifted, hyperactive, or in single-parent homes.

INTRODUCTION

This study is for moms and dads . . . those of us engaged in the exacting and often frustrating task of rearing children. If you are like me, you are weary of theories and seminars and sermons that sound good but prove unrealistic.

What we want is reliable direction—useful and dependable principles from the Scriptures that work. Our great goal is to launch into society secure, mature, confident, and capable young adults who can handle the pressures thrown at them in the demanding arena of life. The home—not the school or the church—is the cutting edge of that process. Home is where the rubber meets the road, where our children are prepared for the future.

I am grateful to my friend, Dr. Joe Temple of Abilene, Texas, for passing on to me his keen insights in rearing children. With his approval, I share some of the same truths he put into print in his book, *Know Your Child*. I appreciate his publisher, Baker Book House, allowing me to use and build upon a few of Dr. Temple's original thoughts.

Equal thanks goes to Dr. Howard Hendricks, my major professor during my days at Dallas Theological Seminary. Germs from his course on "The Christian Home" infected me with the right disease . . . and his life has convinced me that one can actually practice what he preaches.

Our prime source of information comes from the One who originated the whole idea of home and family . . . God Himself. I have simply observed some of the truths He has preserved for us in the Old and New Testaments and applied them to the task of rearing children today. God is the One who brought you and your child together, and He will provide you with the daily wisdom you need to rear your child successfully.

Chuck Swindoll

Chuck Swindoll

PUTTING TRUTH
INTO ACTION

Knowledge apart from application falls short of God's desire for His children. He wants us to apply what we learn so that we will change and grow. This study guide was prepared with these goals in mind. As you go through the following pages, we hope your desire to discover biblical truth will grow as your understanding of God's Word increases, and that you will be encouraged to apply what you've learned.

To assist you in your study, we've included a section called **Living Insights** at the end of each lesson. These exercises will challenge you to study further and to think of specific ways to put your discoveries into action.

On occasion a lesson is followed by a **Digging Deeper** section, which gives you additional information and resources to probe further into some issues raised in that lesson.

There are many ways to use this guide—in personal devotions, group studies, discussions with friends and family, and Sunday school classes. And, of course, it's an ideal study aid when you're listening to its corresponding "Insight for Living" radio series.

To benefit most from this study guide, we would encourage you to consider it a spiritual journal. That's why we've included space in the **Living Insights** for recording your thoughts and discoveries. We hope you'll return to those sections often for review and encouragement as you continue to grow in your walk with Christ.

Lee Hough
Coauthor of Text
Author of Living Insights

You and Your Child

Chapter 1

KNOWING YOUR CHILD
Proverbs 22:6; Psalm 139:13–16

Umbilically tied to each newborn bundle brought home from the hospital is a mixed bag of parental emotions ranging from anticipation to anxiety. Within that bag a nagging question tugs at every Christian parent: "When should I begin to instill a godly character in my child?"

The purpose of this study is to demonstrate that to begin an effective child-training process, you must *know* your child. Understanding your child is essential for molding a godly, healthy character.

Understanding the Training Process

Proverbs 22:6 is key to understanding the process of knowing and raising your child:

> Train up a child in the way he should go,
> Even when he is old he will not depart from it.

It's a familiar verse, but one that too many parents misunderstand.

The Popular Conception of the Training

Many see this verse as a promise: as long as you raise your children right, you don't need to worry if at some point they sow a few wild oats; eventually, like the prodigal, they'll come to their senses, sober up, shape up, and ship back to God. But as popular and comforting as this interpretation might be, it does not square with Scripture, as we will see, nor does it square with our experience.

Experience teaches us that wild oats can make for a painful harvest. Not all prodigals come home. Not all ships return safely to harbor. The bottom of the ocean is strewn with the wreckage of ships that have broken loose from their moorings and strayed from their course, never to return home.

Think of the children who were forced by the determination and strictness of their parents to be in church every Sunday, read

1

the Bible every day, memorize Scripture, read only "Christian" books, and see only "Christian" films. When finally out of the nest, however, the children stretch their wings and immediately fly south to escape such a wintry exposure to Christianity.

This kind of rebellion is deep-seated and is probably aimed not so much at Christianity as at the parents who never won the right to be heard or took the time or trouble to get to know their children as people. Anyone resents being run through an impersonal curriculum and revolts against being treated as a nonperson—and children are no exception. At the center of their being, they want to be *known*, intimately and genuinely, and trained in godliness in a personal way tailor-made for them.

The Nature of the Training

So how do we grasp what Proverbs 22:6 is really saying? Let's begin by looking at the words *train up*. This phrase originally referred to "the palate, the roof of the mouth, the gums." In the verb form, the word depicted placing a rope in the mouth of a wild horse and thereby taming it so it could receive direction. It was also used to describe the action of a midwife, who would dip her fingers into the juice of crushed dates and reach into the newborn's mouth, massaging its gums and palate, creating in the child a desire for sucking. Then she would place the baby in the mother's arms to begin nursing.

Like that shrewd but tender midwife, parents are to not only tame and direct the child's will, but also to create a thirst for the nourishing flow of the parents' wisdom and counsel.

The Duration of the Training

Two words in verse 6 help survey the parameters of the training in terms of time. The word *child* calls to mind a little one, perhaps between infancy and school age. However, the Scriptures use the term in a broader sense, ranging anywhere from a newborn to a person of marriageable age.[1]

---

1. Although translated differently at times, the same Hebrew word for *child* is used in many different passages. For example, in 1 Samuel 4:21, *child* is translated as *boy* in reference to a newborn infant. In Exodus 2:2–3, *child* is used to describe three-month-old Moses. In 1 Samuel 1:22, it is used of Samuel before he was weaned. In Genesis 21:12–20, the translation *lad* is used to refer to Ishmael, a preteen. In Genesis 37:2, *youth* is used of Joseph at age seventeen. And in Genesis 34:19, *young man* is used of a boy of marriageable age.

"Even when he is old he will not depart from it . . ." In the second half of the verse, the root meaning of the Hebrew word for *old* is "bearded" or "chin." Solomon is not envisioning a seventy-year-old prodigal returning home. A boy starts growing a beard when he approaches maturity. Solomon's point is that, in general, when children reach maturity they will not depart from the way they were trained. Therefore, the responsibility of the parents is to continue the training the entire time their children are under their care.

The Implementation of the Training

The manner of training is suggested by the word *in*. This term means "in keeping with, in cooperation with, in accordance to something." The literal rendering is "according to his way." That's altogether different from *your* way, *your* plan, *your* idea, *your* curriculum. The verse doesn't mean "train up a child as you think he should go." Rather, "If you want your training to be meaningful and wise, be observant and discover your child's way, and adapt your training accordingly."

Strengthening this idea is the word *way*. The Hebrew term literally means "road" or "path." Metaphorically, it is "a characteristic." Therefore, the thought is "train up a child in keeping with his characteristics." And his or her characteristics are distinct and set. There is a bent already established within every child God places in our care.[2] Each is not a pliable lump of clay but has been bent according to a predetermined pattern.

For example, if you have several children in your home, one may be creative while another is practical. One may be intelligent; another, less strong academically. One may be outgoing; another, shy. Whatever the case, they're all individuals. They weren't created on the assembly line. They were handcrafted, individually, by God. Consider Jacob and Esau. Esau hunted and loved the outdoor life. Jacob was a mama's boy. Both were individuals; each had his own individual bents. The shortsighted parent, however, overlooks this and focuses only on the immediate task of making the child conform and shape up. The result? When the parent starts yelling "shape up or ship out," the child starts saving up for a boat ticket.

2. The basic concept of the Hebrew verb for *way*, *darak*, has to do with setting foot on territory or objects. In Psalm 7:12 the word is used of God, who "has bent His bow and made it ready." That is, He has set His foot on the bow in order to bend it and string it. In a similar way, God puts His foot on the physical, psychological, and personality bows of our lives to bend them in specific ways.

Parents commonly make two other mistakes. First, they use the same approach with all their children. Second, they compare them with other children. Both mistakes stem from not truly knowing their children, from failing to see their individual bents. Consequently, the crucial concern for us as parents is to understand what the bents are in each of our children so that we can guide them in a way to which they can respond, rather than chaffing under the bit of our training.

Understanding Your Child's Nature

For parents who want to better know their children, an important step is to familiarize themselves with the following three principles.

A General Bent toward Good

Coined in the image of God, each child bears a certain imprint of divinity (Gen. 1:26–27). From this, each person derives a dignity and worth that is to be recognized and protected (compare Gen. 9:6; James 3:8–10). The child also has been given a unique personality and distinctive abilities that God intends him to use for carrying out personalized acts of goodness.

A General Bent toward Evil

Like Midas in reverse, Adam's touch on us all has turned the luster of God's image into tarnish (Rom. 5:12). Each of us, to use C. S. Lewis' words, is born "a Son of Adam or a Daughter of Eve,"[3] not a child of God. Sin's poison passes from generation to generation through the bloodstream of humanity. As a result, each child's spirit is brought into the world stillborn. The only remedy is to be "born again" (John 3:3). This paraphrase of Psalm 51:5 sums up this bent toward evil:

> Behold, I was brought forth [in a state of] iniquity,
> my mother was sinful who conceived me [and I too
> am sinful]. (AMPLIFIED)

Psalm 58:3 conveys the same thought:

> The wicked are estranged from the womb;
> These who speak lies go astray from birth.

---

3. C. S. Lewis, *The Lion, the Witch and the Wardrobe* (New York, N.Y.: Macmillan Publishing Co., Collier Books, 1950), p. 10.

And our experience confirms these truths. You have to instruct children to tell the truth, but you never have to sit down and teach them to lie. That's part of our bent. It comes naturally. If you fail to understand this bent toward evil, inherited from Adam, you will fail to understand the spiritual battle in general and your child in particular.

A Specific Bent toward Evil

Aside from their roots in Adam, all children have a specific bent toward evil which is passed on by their immediate family (Exod. 34:7). In some strange pattern of living peculiar to each family, sin and its effects pass through the family tree like sap. This will be dealt with in depth in chapter 2.

Understanding Your Child's Uniqueness

In addition to the general bents toward good and evil, Psalm 139 tells us that children are endowed with several unique characteristics at birth.[4]

> For Thou didst form my inward parts;
> Thou didst weave me in my mother's womb.
> I will give thanks to Thee, for I am fearfully and
>   wonderfully made;
> Wonderful are Thy works,
> And my soul knows it very well.
> My frame was not hidden from Thee,
> When I was made in secret,
> And skillfully wrought in the depths of the earth.
> Thine eyes have seen my unformed substance;
> And in Thy book they were all written,
> The days that were ordained for me,
> When as yet there was not one of them.
>   (vv. 13–16)

4. In Ecclesiastes, Solomon looks at the development of the child within the womb as one of the great mysteries of life (11:5). Some stunning examples of fiber-optic photography that display the process of development within the womb can be found in the book *A Child Is Born*, rev. ed., by Lennart Nilsson (New York, N.Y.: Dell Publishing, 1989). For illustrations and spiritual applications of Psalm 139 from a doctor's perspective, consult *Fearfully and Wonderfully Made*, by Dr. Paul Brand and Philip Yancey (Grand Rapids, Mich.: Zondervan Publishing House, 1980); and for a week-by-week devotional study of the developing baby, see *The Miracle of Life: Devotions for Expectant Mothers*, by Ken Gire and Dr. Robert G. Wells (Grand Rapids, Mich.: Zondervan Publishing House, 1993).

Let's examine this psalm section by section and see what it reveals about three distinct aspects of your child's uniqueness.

The Emotional Structure of Your Child Is Unique

The phrase *inward parts* (v. 13), which literally means "kidney" in Hebrew, was used to refer to the emotional structure of the individual, the "seat of the tenderest, most secret emotions."[5] In our culture, we refer to the heart in a similar manner. God forms the inner emotional structure of each individual, whether tender-hearted or coolly reasonable, whether deeply reproved by a stern look or barely moved by a week of detention. He makes us as we are for a reason.

The Physical Structure of Your Child Is Unique

Another aspect of a child's uniqueness is revealed in the word *weave*, which means "to knit together into a mass or thicket." With that embryonic ball of yarn, God knits together each child. In the fourteenth verse, after reflecting on this thought, David praises God: "I will give thanks to Thee, for I am fearfully and wonderfully made." Then he continues the anatomy lesson in verse 15:

> My frame [literally, skeleton or bony structure] was
>   not hidden from Thee,
> When I was made in secret,
> And skillfully wrought in the depths of the earth.

The phrase translated "skillfully wrought" is used in Exodus to describe the curtains for the Tabernacle. They were to be made and fitted, formed, and embroidered together so that the tapestry exemplified beauty. Like fine needlepoint, we are put together by God with care and craft.

"In secret . . . in the depths of the earth" is an idiom for "a place of protection, concealment." It's a figurative, poetic way of describing the womb. In that protected and concealed place, God oversees our prenatal development.

---

5. C. F. Keil and F. Delitzsch, *Commentary on the Old Testament in Ten Volumes: Volume 5—Psalms*, 3 vols. in one, trans. James Martin (reprint; Grand Rapids, Mich.: William B. Eerdmans Publishing Co., 1982), vol. 5, p. 349. Both the "kidneys" and the "heart" are tried by God (Ps. 7:9).

The Structure of Your Child's Life Span Is Unique

A third God-given distinctive about each child is introduced in verse 16: "Thine eyes have seen my unformed substance." "Unformed substance" is used in the Talmud to indicate every kind of raw material, like a block of wood or lump of clay. When applied to a human vessel, it would be equivalent to the word *embryo*. The word *seen* means "watched over" in an active sense—as architects painstakingly watch over the construction of a building they have drawn. God has a plan in His mind for each child and watches over that gestation period to the extent that even the days of the child's life are prescribed:

> And in Thy book they were all written,
> The days that were ordained for me,
> When as yet there was not one of them.

Conclusion

The psalmist wants you to realize that the sovereign God of heaven has given you a very special gift. He has planned and arranged for your child to have a specific set of attributes and abilities and a unique personality—as well as a specific limit to his or her days. Make the most of those days, won't you? Get off on the right foot by getting to *know* the child God has so graciously entrusted to you.

Living Insights   STUDY ONE

If anyone can identify with Paul's anguished cry in Rom. 7:15, "I am not practicing what I would like to do, but I am doing the very thing I hate," it's a parent. Just about every mom and dad comes to the task of raising children wanting to practice the right things, only to end up in the middle of an exasperating moment doing and saying the very things they hate, perhaps the very things that were done to them when they were little—the very things they swore they would never do.

Every caring parent hates that. We hate what it does to our children; and we know what it does because we can still remember how terrible we felt when our parents did those same things to us. And we hate ourselves—for hurting them with abusive words, for bullying them with a belittling tone, and for frightening them with an anger that's often menacingly violent and viciously meant to be so. All that, just so we can win.

Is it worth it, all that meanness and hurt hurled back and forth just to win? Never. There has to be a better way to raise a child— a way that doesn't pit mother against daughter or father against son as desperate enemies, ruining one another's lives in the slow increments of day-to-day carping and insults.

That better way begins with knowing our children. Even though that may sound simple, perhaps even ridiculous at first, it is one of the toughest tasks to which we can commit ourselves. Do you know your son or daughter? Really? Often, people only know the mold they're trying to make their children fit into and not the children themselves. Wise parents, however, take pains to observe how God has handcrafted their children, listen to their hurts and hopes, and then, with Jesus' help, train them to walk in His way according to their particular bents. If we fail to know our children, no amount of training—even if it's biblical—is likely to be successful.

Starting today, and for the rest of this series of studies, make a concentrated effort to know your children better. Who are those children He has given you? Ask yourself, What is she like? How would I describe his character bents? What unique qualities do I see in her? In what ways is he different from his brothers or sisters? You might take into consideration what your closest friends perceive in your children, or what their teachers, grandmother, or granddad see. Last, don't forget the children. What do they say about themselves? Are you listening?

Use the following charts to draw a composite of the emotional, intellectual, physical, and spiritual bents in each of your children.

Child's Name: _____	
Evidence of Good Bents	Evidence of Bad Bents

Child's Name: _____

Evidence of Good Bents	Evidence of Bad Bents

Child's Name: _____

Evidence of Good Bents	Evidence of Bad Bents

Child's Name: _____

Evidence of Good Bents	Evidence of Bad Bents

Living Insights

How would you like to apply some of what you've learned from the lesson and get to know your child better at the same time? If you're game, then try this: First, personalize the verses of Psalm 139:13–16 to form a prayer about your son or daughter. You can do this by simply inserting his or her name in the first blank and then filling out the rest with whatever names and pronouns are appropriate.

Then, choose a quiet, restful time when you can be alone with this child and tell him or her you have a special prayer from the Scriptures you'd like to say for them. Read Psalm 139:13–16 from the Living Bible, just as it is written, to familiarize them with it. Then pray your personalized version.

> Father,
> You made all the delicate, inner parts of _____'s body, and knit them together in mother's womb. Thank you for making _____ so wonderfully complex! It is amazing to think about. Your workmanship is marvelous—and how well I know it. You were there while _____ was being formed in utter seclusion! You saw _____ before _____ was born and scheduled each day of _____'s life before _____ began to breathe. Every day was recorded in your Book!

Afterwards, let your child know that you want to understand and know him or her better; that already you've been thinking about how he or she reveals God's wonderful workmanship. Finally, cite some of the good traits you see and tell how much you appreciate them. Let your child marvel at the reflection in the mirror of your praise. Don't criticize or suggest changes. No sermons or comparisons. Just give honest, sincere praise.

Chapter 2

BREAKING GRANDDAD'S BENT

Exodus 34:5–8; Selected Scriptures

Physicians tell us that certain diseases and predispositions to disease are often hereditary. Psychiatrists state that mental illnesses and emotional problems are also sometimes inherited. It stands to reason, then, that certain spiritual characteristics may also be passed down from generation to generation.

This spiritual legacy has three major aspects. First, every person is born in the image of God, with a God-given personality and distinct abilities (Gen. 1:26–27). Second, every person is born with a sin nature, a general bent toward evil inherited from Adam (Rom. 5:12). And third, each of us has a *specific* bent or tendency toward evil handed down from our immediate forefathers. It is this third area that we're going to investigate in this chapter.

The Consequences of Inherited Sin

To start our investigation, let's go back in time. A long way back, to the book of Exodus.

In Exodus 34:5–8, amid the clefts of Mount Sinai, Moses brushed against God's glory in an awesome daybreak encounter.

> And the Lord descended in the cloud and stood there with him as he called upon the name of the Lord. Then the Lord passed by in front of him and proclaimed, "The Lord, the Lord God, compassionate and gracious, slow to anger, and abounding in lovingkindness and truth; who keeps lovingkindness for thousands, who forgives iniquity, transgression and sin; yet He will by no means leave the guilty unpunished, visiting the iniquity of fathers on the children and on the grandchildren to the third and fourth generations." And Moses made haste to bow low toward the earth and worship.

Glinting in the morning sun, the foreboding edge of God's revelation catches our eye: ". . . visiting the iniquity of fathers on the children and on the grandchildren to the third and fourth generations."[1] The term *iniquity* is from a Hebrew word meaning "to bend, to twist, to distort, to pervert." In Proverbs 12:8, it is translated "perverse." Consequently, we could read the passage this way: ". . . visiting the bent, the twisting distortions, the perversions of the fathers on the children and on the grandchildren to the third and fourth generations."

At first glance, this seems vengeful and unfair. Yet, the opposite is true. God could have allowed that same perversion or bent to continue throughout history, fraying or destroying the entire family line. But God says, "No—it will have rippling effects *only* to the third and fourth generations."[2] The scales, then, are weighted not on God's harshness but on His kindness, demonstrating that He is indeed compassionate, gracious, and abounding in loving-kindness for thousands.

The Lord will forgive iniquity, transgression, and sin if and when it is dealt with. If confessed, there is cleansing (1 John 1:9). If not, a terrible price will be exacted, and our children and our children's children will also be the ones who will pay. Proverbs 28:13 instructs us that the response we have to our own sin tips the balance as to whether justice or mercy will be measured out to us:

> He who conceals his transgressions will not prosper,
> But he who confesses and forsakes them will find
> compassion.

A General Example of Inherited Sin

The books of Kings and Chronicles document the civil war that split the nation of Israel into two kingdoms. The southern kingdom was ruled by Solomon's son Rehoboam. The reins to the northern kingdom, however, were given to the wicked Jeroboam, Solomon's trusted servant, who spurred on the nation to runaway sinfulness.

---

1. This phrase, stated almost identically, was first introduced in the giving of the Ten Commandments in Exodus 20:5.

2. "But when, on the other hand, the hating ceases, when the children forsake their fathers' evil ways, the warmth of the divine wrath is turned into the warmth of love . . . and this mercy endures not only to the third and fourth generation, but to the thousandth generation, though only in relation to those who love God, and manifest this love by keeping His commandments." C. F. Keil and F. Delitzsch, *Commentary on the Old Testament in Ten Volumes: Volume 1—The Pentateuch*, 3 vols. in one, trans. James Martin (reprint; Grand Rapids, Mich.: William B. Eerdmans Publishing Co., 1980), vol. 2, pp. 117–18.

Time after time in Kings and Chronicles we read that the nation walked "in the way of Jeroboam" (see 1 Kings 15:34; 16:26). Generations followed his steps into sins of idolatry, immorality, and rebellion. Like three thorny vines, these bents grew out from Jeroboam and inextricably entangled themselves in the nation—until, at last, God had to brandish the pruning shears of judgment (see 1 Kings 14).

A Specific Example of Inherited Sin

Turning back the pages of Israel's history even further, we'll follow a specific bent—deception—through four generations.

In Abraham's Life

Abraham's propensity to shade the truth is brought to light in Genesis 20:

> Now Abraham journeyed from there toward the land of the Negev, and settled between Kadesh and Shur; then he sojourned in Gerar. And Abraham said of Sarah his wife, "She is my sister." So Abimelech king of Gerar sent and took Sarah. But God came to Abimelech in a dream of the night, and said to him, "Behold, you are a dead man because of the woman whom you have taken, for she is married." Now Abimelech had not come near her; and he said, "Lord, wilt Thou slay a nation, even though blameless? Did he not himself say to me, 'She is my sister'? And she herself said, 'He is my brother.' In the integrity of my heart and the innocence of my hands I have done this." (vv. 1–7)

In His merciful justice, God eased Abimelech out of the snare (vv. 6–8), after which the ruffled and flustered king tracked Abraham down to demand an explanation (vv. 9–10). Abraham responded by tailoring a hasty rationalization into a loose-fitting apology:

> "Because I thought, surely there is no fear of God in this place; and they will kill me because of my wife. Besides, she actually is my sister, the daughter of my father, but not the daughter of my mother, and she became my wife; and it came about, when God caused me to wander from my father's house, that I said to her, 'This is the kindness which you

will show to me: everywhere we go, say of me, "He is my brother."'" (vv. 11–13)

She was not only his half sister, she was also his wife. Had Abraham lied like this only once, we might not think much about it. However, when we read in Genesis 12:10–20 that he had told the same lie before, we have to admit that Abraham had a bent toward lying.

In Isaac's Life

As Abraham's family tree spreads its branches, we see the seeds of this trait crop up in the second generation. The bent of lying sprouts in Isaac's life through a situation similar to the one his father had experienced years earlier.

> So Isaac lived in Gerar. When the men of the place asked about his wife, he said, "She is my sister," for he was afraid to say, "my wife," thinking, "the men of the place might kill me on account of Rebekah, for she is beautiful." And it came about, when he had been there a long time, that Abimelech king of the Philistines looked out through a window, and saw, and behold, Isaac was caressing his wife Rebekah. Then Abimelech called Isaac and said, "Behold, certainly she is your wife! How then did you say, 'She is my sister'?" And Isaac said to him, "Because I said, 'Lest I die on account of her.'" And Abimelech said, "What is this you have done to us? One of the people might easily have lain with your wife, and you would have brought guilt upon us." (26:6–10)

In Jacob's Life

Continuing unchecked, the like-father-like-son legacy of deceit then passed from Isaac to his son Jacob. At an early age, Jacob began to develop a Machiavellian habit of doing whatever he needed in order to gain the advantage, no matter how manipulative or mercenary (see 25:27–34).[3] Encouraged by his mother, this habit culminated in an outrageous deception committed against his father.

---

3. Jacob's name literally means "supplanter." *Webster's New Universal Unabridged Dictionary*, 2d ed., defines *supplant* as "to take the place of; to supersede, especially through force, scheming, or treachery."

In what he thought were his dying days, Isaac summoned Jacob's fraternal twin brother, Esau, to go into the field, hunt game, and prepare a last meal for him so "that I may eat, so that my soul may bless you before I die" (27:1–4). Rebekah overheard this and conspired with Jacob, plotting to take advantage of Isaac's poor eyesight and Esau's absence in the field (vv. 5–17). In a treacherous act of repeated deception, Jacob masqueraded as his brother and obtained the blessing for himself (vv. 18–29). And so deception continued to unravel Abraham's tight-knit family until it was a snarl of tangled values and relationships.

In Jacob's Sons

Tragically, the seeds of deception so deeply rooted in Jacob's life became firmly planted in his sons. Like his parents, he also had a favorite child, Joseph. But the other sons resented this, and in a jealous rage, they sold Joseph to a slave caravan headed for Egypt. To cover their crime, they took Joseph's distinctive, multicolored garment, dipped it in animal's blood, and brought it to their father, explaining, "We found this; please examine it to see whether it is your son's tunic or not" (37:32). That was the spoken lie. They hadn't found it; the whole scene, props and all, had been staged. The second lie was unspoken. Jacob examined the garment and said: "It is my son's tunic. A wild beast has devoured him; Joseph has surely been torn to pieces!" (v. 33). And the brothers didn't say a word. They simply stood there, and by their silence, they lied. Like father, like sons.

Short-circuiting the Consequences of Inherited Sin

By now, you're probably asking yourself how you can trip the breaker on those bents and short-circuit the process at work in your own family. You can take several steps to help your children come to terms with their character traits.

First, *introduce your child to Jesus Christ.* The first and biggest step in straightening out these bents is for your child to become aligned to Him who is "the way, and the truth, and the life" (John 14:6). Only through faith in Christ can we be reborn with a new nature that will enable us to choose life over these destructive family bents.

Second, *pray for insight into your child's character.* Remember, to a large degree, your child is a reflection of you. Insight into your character may lead to insight into your child. So apply the words of the psalmist both to you and to your child, and pray that God will "lead [you] in the everlasting way" (Ps. 139:23–24).

Third, *become a student of your child.* Observe your child's words (Luke 6:45) and actions (1 Tim. 5:25), because they reflect character . . . or the lack of it.

Fourth, *be consistent.* It takes great diligence to weed out those stubborn evil bents in our children. But beyond simply uprooting the bad, parents must consistently nurture a child's good bents if they are to flourish.

Fifth, *maintain open and loving communication with your family.* You will never know your child unless you take control of your schedule and plan time to listen and observe. This may require putting the TV to bed early instead of the children. Or how about taking on a hobby your child would enjoy and that the two of you could do together? Whatever it takes, your child is worth it!

Living Insights

As any adult knows, straightening out inherited bents toward evil isn't easy. First, you've got to be able to identify them, and that's not always as simple as it sounds. Why? Because oftentimes, nobody in the family really sees a bent that's been around for a generation or two as being all that evil. It becomes an accepted trait, one that defines the family just as much as freckles and flat feet do. As children, then, we blindly accept that bent as being normal, for it is normal in our world. It becomes as natural to us as breathing, and so the bent finds a home for generations.

Until now. Now it's time to identify that kink in your character, time to cut that rotten fruit out of your family tree. It could be a problem with alcoholism, tolerated with the family excuse, "Well, you know us Beckers, we just can't hold our liquor." Or maybe a propensity for cheating; "You want to be a Mitchell, don't you, son? Then get out there and win!" What Dad's actually saying is, "Son, you have my permission to lie, cheat, do whatever it takes to win. And you'd better win if you want to be accepted and loved by this family." So you do. Or perhaps it's a bent toward sexual promiscuity—"boys will be boys"—or to being judgmental, materialistic, violently angry, cruel, sarcastic . . . and the list goes on.

Are you ready to clean house? Then start by taking a hard look at the one you grew up in. And a great way of doing that is through the eyes of your spouse or a longtime friend. They can often discern the bents in our upbringing that we can't. Talk it over, think about it, and try to identify at least two bents toward evil passed down to you that you can target for extinction.

Evil Bents

_____

_____

_____

_____

_____

_____

_____

_____

_____

_____

_____

_____

_____

*L**iving** **I**nsights*   STUDY TWO

Once you've identified the bents you want to get rid of, why not talk about them with your children? It might become a wonderful catalyst for drawing everyone closer together.

Try this: Draw a large family tree on a piece of paper or construction board. Instead of filling in the names of ancestors, write down two bents toward evil that you're wanting to prune out, as well as the Christlike fruits of the Spirit you see being passed down through the family and that you want your children to inherit from you. (Note the sample Family Tree we've created on the next page.)

17

Integrity
Forgiveness   Faith
                        Humility
Arrogance   Steadfastness   Mercy
                    Joy
        Giving
Helpfulness   Self-control   Lying
                        Patience

   To introduce this concept to your children, you might point out some of the physical traits your parents passed on to you and that you handed down to them. For example, a strong chin, green eyes, curly hair, long legs, or knobby knees. From there it should be easy to show them the tree and talk about the bents toward good and evil that get passed on in a family as well. Have them go over each limb and decide which ones need pruning and which need nurturing.

   At this point, be prepared to ask your children to forgive you for the ways you may have already been passing destructive traits on to them. You might also want to talk about some of the ways you see yourself doing this and how you plan to stop.

   Last, pray with your son or daughter and ask for Jesus' strength and grace in removing these bent branches from your family tree.

Chapter 3

LOVING YOUR CHILD
Psalms 127:1–128:3

Looking back to when you were a child, how many of you felt genuinely loved by your parents?"

When that question was asked of sixteen people in a Bible study group, most of whom had been raised in Christian homes, only two raised their hands—and one was reluctant at that!

As they expanded on why they had not felt loved, several poured out answers such as:

- "He was too busy for me."

- "She never really understood me—didn't even try!"

- "I wasn't important to him. I got in his way."

- "Our family had everything in the way of material possessions, but nothing in the way of love."

Many of us can identify with what they said. Too many. And it's more than a little unnerving to be parents ourselves now, responsible for cultivating the kind of loving relationships with our children that we never experienced.

In this study of Psalms 127 and 128, we will see a vibrant domestic mural unfold that chronicles the development of a close, healthy family. That mural will serve as a pattern for us to follow so that when our children are later asked, "Did you feel loved by your parents when you were little?" they'll enthusiastically answer, "*Yes!*"

A Panoramic View

The mural revealed in Psalms 127 and 128 traces four distinct seasons of family life. The beginning of a home is painted in Psalm 127:1–2. The expansion of the home is portrayed in verses 3–5. The training in the home is pictured in Psalm 128:1–3. And finally, the blessings of the later years—when the children have left—are seen in verses 4–6.

Let's step up and closely examine the verbal brush strokes in the first three scenes of family life.

First Scene: The Beginning of the Home

The opening verse of Psalm 127 pictures the foundation for a strong and stable home.

> Unless the Lord builds the house,
> They labor in vain who build it;
> Unless the Lord guards the city,
> The watchman keeps awake in vain.
> (v. 1)

In Old Testament times, the construction of a city was not even begun until surrounding protective walls were in place. But the walls could only provide so much security. After all, they could be scaled, burned, or knocked down. So, ultimately, the people needed to have God as their fortress of trust, not their walls or the watchmen (see Prov. 18:10).

The same is true for our families. Unless a husband and wife build their lives on their trust in God, their work and watchfulness are wasted. Because, like Jericho's walls, their efforts can come tumbling down as quick as a shout.

Many, unfortunately, feel that they can bypass this foundational trust, trying instead to build a stronger home by working harder and longer hours. But verse 2 of Psalm 127 dispels that mistaken notion.

> It is vain for you to rise up early,
> To retire late,
> To eat the bread of painful labors;
> For He gives to His beloved even in his sleep.

Burning the candle at both ends—rising early, retiring late—is futile. It is God's blessing, not our painful labors to provide better things for our families, that establishes a home. Our trust should be in His hand over our home, not in the feverish frenzy of our own hands.

Second Scene: The Expansion of the Home

A perfect illustration of one of God's blessings is children. And with their presence comes the birth of a new stage in the home— the expansion years. Solomon presents several pictures of this scene to us, the first found in verse 3a:

> Behold, children are a gift of the Lord.

The Hebrew word for *gift* means "property" or "possession." From a divine viewpoint, your children are not your own; they are God's property. He has appointed you as their stewards, entrusting them to your care and bestowing them for your enjoyment for a brief period of time.

In the second half of verse 3, Solomon fashions another image to describe children:

The fruit of the womb is a reward.

A child is not simply a tax deduction, another mouth to feed, an inconvenient demand on life. He or she is a reward, potentially luscious fruit. But luscious fruit doesn't just happen. It is cultivated by a diligent farmer who tills, sows, waters, fertilizes, weeds, and prunes. This metaphor conveys the idea that child-rearing takes time, care, nurturing, and cultivation. It suggests an attitude of attention rather than neglect, interest rather than irritation. The only things that grow well untended are weeds. So, just as the harvest is the farmer's reward, so children are the parents' reward. And our expressions of love and acceptance toward them should reflect that truth.

The next picture on the mural is found in verses 4–5.

Like arrows in the hand of a warrior,
So are the children of one's youth.
How blessed is the man whose quiver is full of
     them;
They shall not be ashamed,
When they speak with their enemies in the gate.

The image of the arrow tells us something about parenting: skill in handling the arrow is crucial. When God specifically designs and places arrows in a couple's quiver, wise parents will draw them out, examine them, and understand them—before they launch them into the world. And it won't be easy. Child-rearing, like archery, is difficult to master. Parents must learn how to position the arrow on the bow, how much tension to place on the string, how to aim the arrow, how to adjust for wind and distance, and finally, how to release the arrow so that it will strike the target.

Third Scene: The Training in the Home

As scenes shift from expansion to training in the first three verses of Psalm 128, we encounter another visual description of a home happy with children.

How blessed is everyone who fears the Lord,
Who walks in His ways.
When you shall eat of the fruit of your hands,
You will be happy and it will be well with you.
Your wife shall be like a fruitful vine,
Within your house,
Your children like olive plants
Around your table.

Notice again how central the Lord is to a home's happiness. Through Him our labors will bring us enjoyment (v. 2). Through Him wives will be a source of beauty and life in the home (v. 3a). And through Him children will flourish like olive trees, which generously provide food, oil, and shelter for others (v. 3b).

Interestingly, the original Hebrew text reads, "Your children will be like *transplanted* olive shoots." At the end of the nine months within the greenhouse of the womb, God takes those tender seedlings and transplants them into our care. Then it becomes our responsibility to attend to them, cultivate them, love them, and train them up to be like

a tree firmly planted by streams of water,
Which yields its fruit in its season,
And its leaf does not wither.
(Ps. 1:3)

Four Areas of Stumbling . . . Four Areas of Love

In Matthew 18, Jesus gives us an incredible glimpse into how God regards children, crystallizing some of the finer points we've seen in our mural of Psalms 127 and 128. Most importantly, He says,

"Whoever receives [or welcomes] one such child in
My name receives Me." (v. 5)

Stated simply, this verse is saying that our attitude toward our children reveals our attitude toward God. Awesome thought, isn't it? But there's more—consider Jesus' words of warning in the next verse:

"But whoever causes one of these little ones who
believe in Me to stumble, it is better for him that a
heavy millstone be hung around his neck, and that
he be drowned in the depth of the sea." (v. 6)

Sobering words. For parents struggling to overcome the deficiencies of their own upbringing, it is easy to unconsciously drop a few stumbling blocks in your little ones' paths. To help you avoid this destructiveness, here are a few common stumbling blocks to keep your eye out for. With God's help, these can be smoothed into ways of blessing.

First: The Way We Listen to Our Children

The way we listen to our children reveals either a lack of interest or the presence of it. Not listening to a child, however young or old, is one of the surest ways of killing a budding relationship. Children feel the need to be heard just as intensely as adults. And though their thinking may be simplistic or immature or even silly, it's crucial to their self-esteem for parents to give them the respect of listening carefully to what they have to say.

Mom, do you stop what you're doing when addressing your children? Dad, do you send busy signals every time one of your children tries to talk to you? Are you both tuned in well enough to your children so that you can hear what they're *not* saying as well as what they do say? Proverbs 20:5 tells us:

> A plan in the heart of a man is like deep water,
> But a man of understanding draws it out.

Listening is not a passive activity; it's work. It's seeking to understand, asking questions for clarification, asking questions to draw out the deep waters that children often have trouble expressing. That's listening.

Second: The Way We Talk to Our Children

The way we talk to our children reveals either a lack of courtesy or the presence of it. It's heartrending the way many parents backhand their children with calloused, harsh words in public. Walk through any mall and you'll hear ugly, sharp, stinging statements made without apology to children whose only real crime is that they're behaving like children. And with each cruel verbal slap, the child withdraws further into a wintry silence that speaks poignantly of the barrenness of the relationship.

When was the last time you heard a parent say something like, "Dear, this afternoon Mom has been really edgy, and I'm very sorry"? Or how about, "Son, I know what I said in front of your friends must have embarrassed you. I shouldn't have said it that way. Will you forgive me?" Or perhaps something as simple as, "That was great, kids! I really appreciate your obeying with such a great attitude"? Every parent should memorize Proverbs 16:24:

Pleasant words are a honeycomb,
Sweet to the soul and healing to the bones.

Children are so tender, so vulnerable to even our tone of voice, let alone to the words we use. Is your speech bringing healing or hurt?

Third: The Way We Discipline Our Children

The way we discipline our children reveals either a lack of compassion and conviction or the presence of it. When it comes to discipline, parents are susceptible to one of two extremes. We can be inconsistent, with not enough faithful discipline, or we can be too severe. Either extreme reduces the chance of there being genuine love between the parent and child. Mom and Dad, be consistent in your training about what's right and what's wrong. Establish clear boundaries and uphold them so that your child will have a secure world in which the two of you can develop a good relationship.

At the same time, guard against going to the other extreme and being abusive verbally or physically. Be compassionate. Don't put adult expectations on children and then berate them miserably for failing. Remember also what James said:

But let everyone be quick to hear, slow to speak and slow to anger; for the anger of man does not achieve the righteousness of God. (James 1:19b–20)

Fourth: The Way We Develop Our Children

The way we nurture our children reveals either a lack of time and involvement or the presence of it. Children cannot develop in isolation. They need their parents' interaction, affirmation, and example; the television, toys, and a constant shuffling of baby-sitters make for poor substitutes.

Many children today who are well clothed and fed are actually starving. What they hunger for is the human touch of their own parents. For too long they've been denied that affection, and their love for Mom and Dad is withering away. The only way to revive that love is through *involvement*. We cannot truly love a child we don't know, nor can we expect that child to love a parent who's never around.

Living Insights

For many parents today, being involved in the development of their children means little more than being a harried taxi driver constantly hurrying to get kids to and from lessons, practices, rehearsals, and games. The home functions like a pinball machine with family members ricocheting off one another as they bounce from one activity to the next. The front door becomes a revolving door, the dining room—a dinosaur, a relic nearing extinction in the age of fast food.

Why? How has this happened? In her excellent book *Traits of a Healthy Family*, Dolores Curran answers:

> Because we bought into that mentality fostered by the fifties that the healthier the family, the more *involved* it was. In fact, involvement was the pivotal word in family life. The healthy family was involved in home, neighborhood, community, church, self-fulfillment, youth leagues, local schools, Jaycees, League of Women Voters—and that's just touching the first layer of possibilities.
>
> We are beginning to sense the error in our fifties thinking and realize that the stress rampant in families today is the ultimate danger in involvement. The 551 family professionals I surveyed tell us, loud and clear, that the healthy family spends more time *together*, and not more time involved in activities that steal members from one another. . . .
>
> What is more valuable for a child—participation in organized activities or the opportunity to live in a family that spends time together? . . . "I see too many kids who had Little League coaches for parents," said a pediatrician. "Why don't their parents realize that if they take the time they spend driving kids to practices and watching games and spend it with their children they all would be better off? How important is playing twelve baseball games

or twenty hockey games to them twenty-five years later when they don't remember having had a family?"[1]

Good question. Do you have the time to think about it? Or do you need to run because Jimmy has soccer at 3:30, Jenny has piano at 4:00, Will needs to be picked up from basketball at 5:30 after you pick up Jenny promptly at 5:00 and Jimmy at 5:15. Then you've got to take Will to church at 6:00, drive across town to make a committee meeting by 7:00, and be back in time to pick him up at 9:00. And that's just on Tuesdays.

See what we mean? Why not redefine the concept of being involved in your children's lives to mean being together? Stop letting activities fragment your family. Sure, they may be fun, but before you sign up for another class, another season, another league or lesson, ask yourself, How will this affect the family? Will it strengthen my involvement with my children or weaken it?

In twenty-five years, will your kids remember having had a family?

Living Insights

Let's get practical about being involved in our children's lives with this one simple assignment: Go play.

Now, that doesn't mean dropping the kids off to play somewhere while you run errands or watch them; it means taking your shoes off and getting in the mud with them. It means working up a sweat wrestling on the living room floor. It means coloring together, playing Marco Polo in a pool, teaching someone how to fish, reading an adventure story, or perhaps pulling a wagonload of little people around the block "just one more time." Whatever the game, you do it together. Close your daily planner, put on your grubbies, take off your watch, disconnect the phone, and have fun.

Your child needs that. He needs that sense of being special that he gets each time you put him on your shoulders. She needs the security that she feels sitting in your lap. They both need the comfort of your presence and the reassurance of your hugs.

---

1. Dolores Curran, *Traits of a Healthy Family* (Minneapolis, Minn.: Winston Press, 1983), pp. 124–25, 139.

But that's the mystery of play, the wonder and power of it. Through the simplest, seemingly ordinary things, we communicate more intangibles about the love we have for our children than all our sermonizing ever could.

So go ahead, get involved with your children—go play. Draw chalk pictures on the sidewalk with your seven-year-old. Times like that aren't a luxury; they're a necessity.

Chapter 4

YOU CAN'T HAVE ONE WITHOUT THE OTHER

Genesis 25–28

A number of years ago, Dr. René Spitz of New York published the shocking results of a study on children confined in two institutions. Both places were identical in every respect—food, housing, hygiene—except one: the amount of affection provided.

In one institution, called "Nursery," the infants were taken care of by their own mothers, who gave them great love, attention, and encouragement. As time passed, these children developed into normal, healthy toddlers. But in "Foundlinghome," the second institution, infants were raised from the third month on by overworked nurses in charge of eight to twelve babies. After two years, these emotionally starved children were unable to speak, walk, or even feed themselves.

In addition, during a five-year period of observation, not one child died in "Nursery," while the mortality rate for just two years in "Foundlinghome" hit 37 percent. Those who did survive, with only one or two exceptions, were "human wrecks."[1]

In a tragically real sense, the clear message communicated by the listless faces of those love-starved children is this—we love or we perish. Love is essential for human development, which means it is essential for a happy, healthy home. You can't have one without the other. The absence of love or the wrong type of love in a home can produce heartbreaking results.[2]

Some Selective Parents

A case in point is the foundering home of Isaac and Rebekah. They loved their sons Jacob and Esau, but with a conditional love that brought its own heartbreaking results.

---

1. See Ashley Montague, "A Scientist Looks at Love," *Phi Delta Kappan*, May 1970, pp. 464–65.

2. For further study on the essentialness of love, see Proverbs 10:12; 13:24; and 15:17.

Selective in Their Love

Let's go back to the time of the twins' birth in Genesis 25 and note the feeling each parent had for them.

> And Isaac prayed to the Lord on behalf of his wife, because she was barren; and the Lord answered him and Rebekah his wife conceived. . . . When her days to be delivered were fulfilled, behold, there were twins in her womb. Now the first came forth red, all over like a hairy garment; and they named him Esau. And afterward his brother came forth with his hand holding on to Esau's heel, so his name was called Jacob; and Isaac was sixty years old when she gave birth to them.
>
> When the boys grew up, Esau became a skillful hunter, a man of the field; but Jacob was a peaceful man, living in tents. Now Isaac loved Esau, because he had a taste for game; but Rebekah loved Jacob. (vv. 21, 24–28)

"Now Isaac loved Esau, because . . ." That one word *because* reveals the true nature of Isaac's love. It was conditional. He didn't love his firstborn simply for who he was, but because Esau "had a taste for game"—he was an outdoorsman. Apparently, Isaac loved the outdoors too, and this mutual interest became the basis of his love for Esau. We can assume that so long as Esau remained a skillful hunter his father could be proud of, so long as they could stalk, track, and trap wild game together, Isaac's love for Esau would remain strong. But let Esau tire of playing the role of the manly huntsman, and he'd quickly find his father's love tiring too.

Now Jacob, of course, was the complete opposite of Esau. He liked staying out of the sun and hanging around the tents. The boy couldn't stand the fierceness of the hunt or the sight of blood—he was "a peaceful man" (v. 27). This is probably why Rebekah's love gravitated toward Jacob. He was around a lot, shared in domestic chores, and was gentle. He appreciated her. Probably, too, Isaac's preference for Esau was obvious, and Rebekah overcompensated for this with Jacob. Possibly, because Esau was the stronger, the most likely to succeed, she became overprotective and continually rallied for her underdog.

Regardless of the motivation, her love wasn't unconditional

either, but possessive and manipulative. In short, Isaac and Rebekah both made their love something that had to be earned. Neither son ever knew what it was like to feel accepted and secure in an unconditional relationship. They grew up always having to perform in order to receive their parents' approval.

Selective in Their Loyalties

In a home where love is conditional, the mother and father, like Rebekah and Isaac, are naturally going to have favorites. And nowhere will these preferences be more visible than in times of family conflict.

In particular, notice the time Rebekah conspired to deceive Isaac into giving to Jacob, instead of to Esau, the family blessing (Gen. 27). The scheme was successful, but Esau retaliated with a threat to kill Jacob (v. 41)—hardly the picture of a happy, healthy home.

Added to this seething caldron of hatred and deception was the bitter grief Esau caused his parents by marrying not one, but two Hittite women (26:34–35). It's probable he took the pagan wives as a deliberate affront to his parents. Neither had sought to know him, understand him, or train him according to his character. Undoubtedly hurt by his father's conditional love and his mother's favoritism toward Jacob, Esau rebelled in the one way he knew would irritate his parents.

Resourceful as ever, though, Rebekah found a way to use Esau's wives to further her plans for Jacob. Knowing that Jacob's life was in danger, she quickly concocted a plan to have him sent to her brother's to be married where he would be safe. Notice how she arranged this by complaining to Isaac about Esau's wives.

> And Rebekah said to Isaac, "I am tired of living because of the daughters of Heth; if Jacob takes a wife from the daughters of Heth, like these, from the daughters of the land, what good will my life be to me?" (27:46)

Isaac did exactly what Rebekah had manipulated him into doing. He called Jacob in and had a good father-son talk. Loosely translated, it might have sounded something like this:

> "Son, if you marry a girl like either of Esau's wives, it will be the death of your mother. The disappointment would just be too much. . . . So I've

30

decided that you should go to Laban's in Paddan-aram and marry one of his daughters. It would really make your mother happy." (see 28:1–3)

Little did Isaac know that Jacob and Rebekah had conspired to have him say this very thing (27:42–45). Jacob probably had his camels already packed. Still, he listened politely as if hearing it all for the first time and then obediently left for Paddan-aram— quickly, before Esau could get ahold of him.

Later, Esau, having heard of Isaac's blessing upon Jacob for marrying "the right kind of girl" from their own people (28:6–7), rushed out to do the same, pathetically hoping that at last he might earn his parents' approval.

> So Esau saw that the daughters of Canaan displeased his father Isaac; and Esau went to Ishmael, and married, besides the wives that he had, Mahalath the daughter of Ishmael, Abraham's son, the sister of Nebaioth. (vv. 8–9)

Poor Esau. Not even this would bring him the elusive prize of his parents' acceptance. For he had unwittingly married into the family of his father's old rival.

Esau's desperate attempt illustrates just how important a parent's love and approval are to a child. Even after having grown up, many men and women still seek from their parents the acceptance they were never given as children.[3]

Some Selective Advice

"Your family is what you've got," writes Peter Collier.

> It's your limits and your possibilities. Sometimes you'll get so far away from it you'll think you're outside its influence forever, then before you figure out what's happening, it will be right beside you, pulling the strings. Some people get crushed by their families. Others are saved by them.[4]

3. For further study on this, read John Trent and Gary Smalley's excellent book, *The Blessing* (Nashville, Tenn.: Thomas Nelson Publishers, 1986).

4. As quoted by Dolores Curran in *Traits of a Healthy Family* (San Francisco, Calif.: Harper and Row, Publishers, 1983), p. 1.

From a strictly human perspective, Collier is right. Esau and Jacob bore the crushing imprint of their parents' conditional love to prove it. But fortunately, family is not all we've got. As believers, we've been reborn into another family, with Almighty God as our heavenly Father. In His loving arms we find our need for unconditional love and acceptance fully, perfectly met. And He can help us heal the wounds of the wrong kinds of love that have been passed down for generations in our families.

So how do we begin anew in our own parenting? How can we break the old habits of withholding love or loving the wrong way? First of all, *there has to be a desire to change.* Without the will, we'll never find the way. Wanting to change is essential. If needed, ask God to create in you an open and willing heart that passionately desires to love His way.

Second, *there must be an admission of our failure.* We can all point to shortcomings in the way we love our children: angry outbursts, vengeful punishment, calloused attitude, or conditional acceptance. Changing these hurtful patterns begins with confessing them before the Lord. Take a moment to read David's confession in Psalm 51:1–17; then personalize it so that it becomes your psalm, your heart that is broken and contrite before God. Then sit down with each of your children individually. Tell them about the specific shortcomings in your love that you confessed to the Lord. Children are the most forgiving people in the world. And they'll love you even more for admitting your problems and wanting to change them.

Third, *there needs to be a plan developed to help you change your habits.* If not, whatever desire for change you have will wane and eventually vanish for lack of direction. Put down on paper whatever changes need to occur in your parenting. Clarify them, break them down, being as specific as possible. Once that's done, let a trusted friend whose wisdom you respect read it—then incorporate their suggestions.

Fourth, *there must be faith and dependence upon the Holy Spirit.* Habits are easily changed on paper, but in real life they're hard to break. Only the Holy Spirit can provide the strength needed to replace our old habits with new ones that conform us to the image of our Father. Remember to commit not only your plans but yourself each day to the Spirit's care and guidance.

"Oh look, Daddy, I catched it!"

That's my boy. Now get ready; here comes another. Make me proud and catch this one too.

"Look, Daddy, I'm only eight years old and I can throw faster than anyone in the league!"

But your batting stinks, Tiger. Can't play in the big leagues if you can't hit.

"Look, Dad, I'm sixteen and already I've made the varsity team."

You better do a little less bragging and a little more practicing on your defense. Still needs a lot of work.

"Look, Father, I'm thirty-five and the company has made me a vice president!"

Maybe someday you'll start your own business like your old man, then you'll really feel a sense of accomplishment.

"Look at me, Bill, I'm forty, successful, well respected in the community, I have a wonderful wife and family—aren't you proud of me now, Dad?

"All my life it seems I've caught everything but that one prize I wanted most—your approval. Can't you say it, Dad? Is it too much to ask for? Just once I'd like to know that feeling every child should have of being loved unconditionally. I'd like for you to put your arm around my shoulders and, instead of telling me I'm not good enough, tell me that in your eyes I'm already a winner and always will be no matter what.

"Look at me, Daddy, I'm all grown up . . . but in my heart still lives a little boy who yearns for his father's love. Won't you pitch me the words I've waited for all my life?

"I'll catch them, Father, I promise."

How can you pass on the powerful legacy of unconditional love and acceptance to your children? Perhaps this story will help.

> During the first day of an introductory speech class, [the] teacher was going around the room, having the students introduce themselves. Each student

was to respond to the questions "What do I like about myself?" and "What don't I like about myself?"

Nearly hiding at the back of the room was Dorothy. Her long, red hair hung down around her face, almost obscuring it from view. When it was Dorothy's turn to introduce herself, there was only silence in the room. Thinking perhaps she had not heard the question, the teacher moved his chair over near hers and gently repeated the question. Again, there was only silence.

Finally, with a deep sigh, Dorothy sat up in her chair, pulled back her hair, and in the process revealed her face. Covering nearly all of one side of her face was a large, irregularly shaped birthmark—nearly as red as her hair. "That," she said, "should show you what I don't like about myself."

Moved with compassion, this godly professor leaned over and gave her a hug. Then he kissed her on her cheek where the birthmark was and said, "That's OK, Honey, God and I still think you're beautiful."

Dorothy cried uncontrollably for almost twenty minutes. . . . When she finally could talk, as she dabbed the tears from her eyes she said to the professor, "I've wanted so much for someone to hug me and say what you said. Why couldn't my parents do that? My mother won't even touch my face."[5]

What lessons about communicating unconditional love to your children can you draw from the professor's actions and words?[6]

_____

_____

_____

_____

_____

5. Gary Smalley and John Trent, *The Blessing* (Nashville, Tenn.: Thomas Nelson Publishers, 1986), pp. 47–48.

6. If you need some more ideas, read Mark 1:40–42 and 10:13–16, looking to see how Jesus communicated love and acceptance to the individuals in these passages.

As you think about your own children individually, are any of these insights lacking in the way you're communicating love and acceptance? If so, how can you incorporate them into your relationships at home beginning today?

_____

_____

_____

_____

_____

Chapter 5

SHAPING THE WILL
WITH WISDOM

Selected Proverbs

In his excellent book *The Strong-Willed Child*, Dr. James Dobson describes the inevitable tug-of-war between the parents' will and the child's.

> It is obvious that children are aware of the contest of wills between generations, and that is precisely why the parental response is so important. When a child behaves in ways that are disrespectful or harmful to himself or others, his hidden purpose is often to verify the stability of the boundaries. This testing has much the same function as a policeman who turns doorknobs at places of business after dark. Though he tries to open doors, he hopes they are locked and secure. Likewise, a child who assaults the loving authority of his parents is greatly reassured when their leadership holds firm and confident. He finds his greatest security in a structured environment where the rights of other people (and his own) are protected by definite boundaries.[1]

The objective in child rearing is not for you as a parent to win the tug-of-war by force, at all costs. For if you do, you may end up not only with a muddy, tearful child but also with a relationship strained beyond repair. Rather, your objective is to shape the child's will, gently yet firmly, as a potter would a clay vase. But that takes a special kind of wisdom—a wisdom only God can provide.

This chapter was not a part of the original series but is compatible with it. It is a revised version of "Shaping the Will with Wisdom," from the study guide *The Strong Family*, coauthored by Ken Gire, with Living Insights written by Lee Hough, from the Bible-teaching ministry of Charles R. Swindoll (Anaheim, Calif.: Insight for Living, 1991).

1. James Dobson, *The Strong-Willed Child* (Wheaton, Ill.: Tyndale House Publishers, 1977), p. 30.

Some Necessary Distinctions worth Making

Nowadays the word *discipline* is emotionally charged. It has been unjustly caricaturized as a synonym for brutalizing children. In addition, the media and popular "expert" opinions have portrayed parents who discipline as Cro-Magnons with clubs. As a result, many people avoid any kind of discipline with their children.

Proverbs, however, tells us that if we truly love our children, we'll discipline them diligently (13:24). Could it be that by neglecting this important aspect of child rearing we are in fact denying our children the instruction and guidance they need to mature into healthy adults? Isn't refusing to teach our children what's right and warn them of what's wrong simply another form of the abuse we call neglect?

Of course it is. We cannot feed and clothe the outer person while ignoring the needs of the inner person and call ourselves good parents. That's why we must discipline our children. But since the subject of discipline is generally such a cloudy one, we need to make some important distinctions that will help clarify the concept.

Between Abuse and Discipline

Abuse is unfair, extreme, and degrading. It's unduly harsh, unnecessarily long, and totally inappropriate. It tears a child's spirit down. When you drag children's feelings through the mud and kick them when they're down, you're being abusive. The result? A soiled self-esteem and scars that often last a lifetime. That's not discipline; it's abuse. And abuse doesn't grow out of love; it stems from hate.

Discipline is fair, fitting, and upholds the child's dignity. Discipline is built on a foundation of justice. It isn't capricious or arbitrary, so the child should have a good idea of the punishment that will be meted out if parental boundaries are willfully and defiantly violated. This form of correction strengthens rather than shatters the child's self-worth; it builds the spirit up. Discipline is rooted in proper motivation—love and genuine concern—not in anger or expedience.

Between Crushing and Shaping

Proverbs 15:13 paints a vivid contrast between a spirit that has been shaped and one that has been crushed:

A joyful heart makes a cheerful face,
But when the heart is sad, the spirit is broken.

Proverbs 17:22 presents a similar image:

A joyful heart is good medicine,
But a broken spirit dries up the bones.

The ultimate goal of discipline is to build up your children with direction and confidence, giving them a strong and secure self-esteem to carry them through life. Shaping the will nurtures a love for life, while crushing the will "dries up" that vitality.

Between Natural Childishness and Willful Defiance

All children need space in which to make mistakes and learn in their early years. As a parent, it's important for you to distinguish between childish irresponsibility and behavior that is willfully disobedient. Again, Dr. Dobson offers insight on the subject.

> A child should not be spanked for behavior that is not willfully defiant. When he forgets to feed the dog or make his bed or take out the trash—when he leaves your tennis racket outside in the rain or loses his bicycle—remember that these behaviors are typical of childhood. It is, more than likely, the mechanism by which an immature mind is protected from adult anxieties and pressures. Be gentle as you teach him to do better. If he fails to respond to your patient instruction, it then becomes appropriate to administer some well-defined consequences (he may have to work to pay for the item he abused or be deprived of its use, etc.). However, childish irresponsibility is very different from willful defiance, and should be handled more patiently.[2]

Several Suggestions worth Considering

Wisely shaping your child's will is a critical task of parenting. Here are some suggestions that should make it easier and more effective.

Start Early

We look again to Proverbs for insight regarding this awesome

2. Dobson, *The Strong-Willed Child*, p. 32.

responsibility. In 13:24 Solomon provides some practical hints:

> He who spares his rod hates his son,
> But he who loves him disciplines him diligently.

The word *diligently* has a colorful background in Hebrew. Orig-inally, it meant "dawn" or "early morning." Later it evolved into the idea of pursuing something early in life—like a career—and thus came to mean "with determination" or "with diligence." The association of *diligence* with *discipline* indicates that we should start disciplining our children early in their lives. The longer we wait to begin the process, the more difficult it will become (compare 19:18).

Stay Balanced

Balance is what keeps children from falling off their bicycles and skinning their knees; it also keeps parents from crashing in their approach to discipline. Two kinds of discipline are mentioned in the Bible. Both complement each other, and both must be kept in balance.

First, let's look at *physical discipline*. Proverbs 22:15 describes this category of discipline.

> Foolishness is bound up in the heart of a child;
> The rod of discipline will remove it far from him.

The rod indicates the infliction of pain. Once again we turn to Dr. Dobson as he underscores the importance of a child being able to associate wrongdoing with pain.

> If your child has ever bumped his arm against a hot stove, you can bet he'll never deliberately do that again. He does not become a more violent person because the stove burnt him; in fact, he learned a valuable lesson from the pain. Similarly, when he falls out of his high chair or smashes his finger in the door or is bitten by a grumpy dog, he learns about physical dangers in his world. These bumps and bruises throughout childhood are nature's way of teaching him what to fear. They do not damage his self-esteem. They do not make him vicious. They merely acquaint him with reality. In like manner, an appropriate spanking from a loving parent provides the same service. It tells him there are not only

physical dangers to be avoided, but he must steer clear of some social traps as well (selfishness, defiance, dishonesty, unprovoked aggression, etc.).[3]

The second kind of discipline is *verbal discipline*. This category of correction, also known as reproof, is found in Proverbs 3:11–12.

My son, do not reject the discipline of the Lord,
Or loathe His reproof,
For whom the Lord loves He reproves,
Even as a father, the son in whom he delights.

Reproof is not a tongue-lashing with cutting remarks that lacerate the spirit. It is verbal instruction arising out of a genuine and deep-felt delight in the child (note the word *delights* in verse 12). Proverbs 29:15 shows verbal reproof in balance with physical discipline: "The rod and reproof give wisdom."

Be Consistent

When you're under pressure, it's easy to let expediency determine how and when you discipline your child—a case of the urgent squeezing out the important. But the rule shouldn't be expediency; it should be consistency. Here are a few guidelines to ensure that your discipline will be consistent.

1. Make sure the rules are known beforehand.

2. Discipline privately.

3. Explain the violation and its consequences.

4. Administer the rod with firmness.

5. Hold your child tenderly after the spanking.

6. Assure your child of your love and concern.

Be Reasonable

As a child grows older, there comes a time when it is inappropriate to use physical punishment. If you're not sensitive to this, you will end up demeaning rather than disciplining your child.

---

3. James Dobson, *Hide or Seek*, rev. ed. (Old Tappan, N.J.: Fleming H. Revell Co., 1979), p. 95.

Significant Goals worth Implementing

You may miss the mark on discipline from time to time, but if you don't have a goal in sight, you're likely to miss every time you try. To stay on target, here are a couple of goals.

For Yourself

Model God's role of authority until your children reach the point where there is a natural transfer of that authority from you to God.

For Your Children

Help them cultivate a healthy respect for themselves and others so that they can be strong enough and secure enough to stand up under the pressures of life.

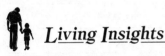 *Living Insights* STUDY ONE

While growing up, many of us came to associate the word *discipline* with only one thing—punishment, usually of the dreaded "wait-till-your-father-gets-home" variety. But as Bruce Ray explains in his book *Withhold Not Correction*, discipline is more than simply punishment.

> Biblical discipline is *correction*, and that means that the pattern of the child's behavior must be *changed by instruction* in righteousness. He must be shown the error of his way, and then directed to the proper path. This requires explanation and instruction. Biblical discipline demands words.[4]

Too many parents rely on punishment alone to discipline their children. By doing that, they're neglecting to give their kids the assistance they need in understanding and applying God's Word to their lives.

How well prepared are you to shape your children's wills with the wisdom of God's Word? Are you training them in the way they should go or simply punishing them for going in the way they shouldn't?

---

4. Bruce A. Ray, *Withhold Not Correction* (Phillipsburg, N.J.: Presbyterian and Reformed Publishing Co., 1978), p. 87.

The book of Proverbs is loaded with nuggets of wisdom to help train in righteousness—to discipline—your children. With the help of a concordance, dig through this gold mine for words like *discipline, child, rod,* and any others you think might be relevant. In the space provided, keep a record of your findings.

Key Word	Wisdom from Proverbs
_____	_____
_____	_____
_____	_____
_____	_____
_____	_____
_____	_____
_____	_____
_____	_____
_____	_____

In addition to your study of Proverbs, here's a chart you might find helpful in bringing your children up in the Lord. Use it as a primer for further study on your own.

God's Will for Our Attitudes[5]

Is . . .	Not . . .	Key Passages
Love	Lust	Mark 12:28–31; Romans 14:13–19; 1 Corinthians 13:1–13; Romans 13:14
Reliance	Independence	Proverbs 3:5–6; Galatians 5:16
Humility	Pride	James 4:6; Philippians 2:5–8
Gratitude	Presumption	Colossians 3:17
Clear Conscience	Guilt	Romans 14:22–23
Integrity	Irresponsibility	Colossians 3:17, 22
Diligence	Laziness	Colossians 3:23
Eagerness	Compulsion	1 Peter 5:2
Generosity	Selfishness	1 Timothy 6:17–19
Submission	Self-advancement	1 Peter 5:5–6
Courage	Cowardice	John 16:33; Matthew 10:26–28
Contentment	Greed	Hebrews 13:5; Philippians 4:11

Living Insights   STUDY TWO

A clear link often exists between how you were disciplined as a child and how you discipline your children. Using the four suggestions made in this study, reflect on how your parents disciplined you.

Were they diligent about beginning discipline early in your life? When did they begin?

5. Garry Friesen, *Decision Making and the Will of God* (Portland, Oreg.: Multnomah Press, 1980), p. 156. Used by permission.

_____

_____

Did they balance the physical and verbal aspects of your discipline? How?

_____

_____

Was the discipline consistent in your home?

_____

_____

How reasonable do you think your parents were? Explain your answer.

_____

_____

If you have children at home, jot down a few ideas about how you can use the suggestions from our study to wisely discipline them. Note especially the areas you feel need to be changed from the way you were brought up.

_____

_____

_____

_____

_____

For further study, read *The New Dare to Discipline* by James Dobson, *The Key to Your Child's Heart* by Gary Smalley, or *How to Really Love Your Child* by Ross Campbell.

Chapter 6

THE MINISTRY
OF THE ROD
1 Samuel 2:12–3:13

Do you remember what we learned in chapter one? Training up your child involves two things: taming something wild and cultivating a taste for something good and nourishing. And since none of this comes naturally to our little ones, it's up to us to introduce and follow through on these two important tasks during their early years in the home.

What happens if we neglect these two aspects of training, never curbing that reckless spirit, never encouraging a taste for things that are wholesome and healthy? We'll find out as we look at Eli, a well-known Old Testament priest who failed to follow these principles— a father who failed to tame his sons and develop in them a taste for the ways of God.

The Seriousness of Rebellion

Like the slow, suffocating fumes of carbon monoxide, the toxin of rebellion steadily seeped into Eli's home. Wait, though—is rebellion really all that serious? Don't all teenagers go through it as a rite of passage?

In order to differentiate between a teen establishing his or her own identity and biblical rebellion, we need to understand how God views rebellion and consider its effect upon a community and society as a whole. Only then can we fully appreciate the serious condition of Eli's family.

In Israel

Although strict and often severe, the Mosaic laws communicated God's unequivocal commitment to holiness for His people. Even in the laws governing the home, God made it clear that He would not tolerate continued, willful rebellion.

> "If any man has a stubborn and rebellious son who will not obey his father or his mother, and when they chastise him, he will not even listen to them,

45

then his father and mother shall seize him, and bring him out to the elders of his city at the gateway of his home town. And they shall say to the elders of his city, 'This son of ours is stubborn and rebellious, he will not obey us, he is a glutton and a drunkard.' Then all the men of his city shall stone him to death; so you shall remove the evil from your midst, and all Israel shall hear of it and fear." (Deut. 21:18–21)

You can't help but flinch at the harshness of the punishment—any compassionate person would. And certainly God took no pleasure in the stoning of young men. How, then, can we understand these verses? By making a few careful observations.

First, this refers not to a young child but an older boy, known for alcoholism. Second, in a case like this, every effort would have been made by the parents to curb their son's rebellion. Discipline would have been administered without success; a young man like this would have proven over the years that he was determined to be incorrigible. And third, only after exhausting all other resources would these parents have resorted to the ultimate punishment of stoning.

Just as white blood cells surround a harmful infection in our bodies, isolating and attacking it until it is destroyed, so the community leaders were to "remove the evil from [their] midst," protecting the health of their community (compare 1 Cor. 5:13). This extreme form of discipline also served as a deterrent—"and all Israel shall hear of it and fear" (Deut. 21:21b).

One final thought concerning this passage before we move on. Often, undisciplined and inconsistent parents turn to God in a crisis and expect Him to do their job. "Lord, straighten out this child, will You?" Certainly He can be called upon for help, but not for taking over. Parenting is the job He has given to us.

In Society

From Eden to the end times, the world has been, and will continue to be, in revolt against God (see Rom. 1:20–21). In response to this, God has opened the floodgates that would restrain the consequences of rebellion:

> And just as they did not see fit to acknowledge God any longer, God gave them over to a depraved mind, to do those things which are not proper, being filled with all unrighteousness, wickedness, greed,

evil; full of envy, murder, strife, deceit, malice; they are gossips, slanderers, haters of God, insolent, arrogant, boastful, inventors of evil, disobedient to parents. (vv. 28–30)

Did you notice the description in verse 30—*disobedient to parents?* Paul uses this same phrase again in the final letter of his life as he warns Timothy of the end times.

But realize this, that in the last days difficult times will come. For men will be lovers of self, lovers of money, boastful, arrogant, revilers, disobedient to parents, ungrateful, unholy. (2 Tim. 3:1–2)

This is the world in which we must live and raise our children. If we are not actively helping to mold them into the image of Christ, be assured they will be molded into the image of the world (see Rom. 12:2). Which image do you want your child to be conformed to?

Five Reasons for Rebellion

Like us, Eli would have surely wanted his sons to be molded after God's holy character, but they ended up conforming to the world instead. Let's take a close look at the five fatal flaws of Eli's parenting style in order to find out why his sons grew up so bent on being disobedient.

At the time of our story in 1 Samuel 2, Eli was Israel's high priest. Following in their father's vocational footsteps, Hophni and Phinehas had also entered the priesthood. But, as we shall see, several tragic differences distinguished their steps from their dad's.

Not Knowing the Lord

The first difference is perhaps the last you would expect.

Now the sons of Eli were worthless men;[1] they did not know the Lord. (1 Sam. 2:12)

Amazing as it may seem, the high priest's sons, who were priests themselves, did not have a relationship with the Lord. They did

---

1. The Greek term for "worthless men" literally means "sons of Belial." In prophetic literature, *Belial* is used to describe Satan or the Antichrist (see 2 Cor. 6:15). *Belial* comes from two Hebrew words meaning "without" and "profit." In Proverbs, the worthless man is equated with the wicked man whose life is characterized by lying (6:12) and digging up evil (16:27).

the work of priests—performing the rituals and speaking the words—but it was empty, a deliberate sham. Trusting in the Lord should have been a prerequisite for their priesthood, but perhaps Eli, as a compromising parent, soft-pedaled their qualifications.

It's evident from the passages describing Eli's ministry that he was a man of integrity, dedicated to the Lord (compare 1:9–18, 2:18–21). But, apparently, he was too busy with the demands at the house of God to be involved in any significant way with his own children in his own house. Consequently, since the cost of commitment wasn't paid during Hophni's and Phinehas' childhood years, the bills all came due in their adulthood.

Tolerating Fleshly Sin

The first entry in the ledger is seen in 1 Samuel 2:12–14.

> Now the sons of Eli were worthless men; they did not know the Lord and the custom of the priests with the people. When any man was offering a sacrifice, the priest's servant would come while the meat was boiling, with a three-pronged fork in his hand. Then he would thrust it into the pan, or kettle, or caldron, or pot; all that the fork brought up the priest would take for himself. Thus they did in Shiloh to all the Israelites who came there.

The priests who served in the house of God were fed by the offerings brought there by the people. However, they weren't allowed to simply pick and choose the best meat for themselves, nor could they go back for seconds. Instead, God allotted them the breast and the right thigh (see Lev. 7:31–34). Hophni and Phinehas, though, weren't used to restraints, and they grabbed for all the meat their forks would hold! But it gets worse, as indicated by the lengthening accounts payable column.

> Also, before they burned the fat, the priest's servant would come and say to the man who was sacrificing, "Give the priest meat for roasting, as he will not take boiled meat from you, only raw." And if the man said to him, "They must surely burn the fat first, and then take as much as you desire," then he would say, "No, but you shall give it to me now; and if not, I will take it by force." Thus the sin of the young

men was very great before the Lord, for the men despised the offering of the Lord. (1 Sam. 2:15–17)

Eli's sons wanted immediate gratification of their desires, and their servants made that plain—"give it to me now" (v. 16). They also wanted their share before the Lord received His—"before they burned the fat" (v. 15). And furthermore, they would allow nothing to stand in the way of those desires being met—"and if not, I will take it by force" (v. 16).

With no correction to restrain them, their ungoverned passion to satisfy the flesh soon extended into sexual gratification.

Now Eli was very old; and he heard all that his sons were doing to all Israel, and how they lay with the women who served at the doorway of the tent of meeting. (v. 22)

They not only practiced immorality, they did it with a brazen and blasphemous arrogance. And Eli did little to stop them.

Failing to Apply Correct Discipline

Aware of his sons' disobedience, Eli makes only an anemic attempt at discipline:

And he said to them, "Why do you do such things, the evil things that I hear from all these people? No, my sons; for the report is not good which I hear the Lord's people circulating. If one man sins against another, God will mediate for him; but if a man sins against the Lord, who can intercede for him?" (vv. 23–25a)

Two mistakes stand out in Eli's response. First, he asked the question *why*, which would only lead to fruitless discussion. He already knew why—because they despised the Lord. Perhaps asking the question was Eli's way of denying the truth of his own failure as a parent. Second, he condemned Hophni and Phinehas on the basis of hearsay. No doubt they were guilty, but Eli should have confronted them when he had the facts, not just secondhand information. Besides, was he that out of touch with his own sons that he hadn't seen for himself what was plain to everyone else?

Failing to Teach Respect for Authority

At the heart of their rebellion was the fact that Hophni and

Phinehas had no respect for authority. This can be seen toward the last half of verse 25: "But they would not listen to the voice of their father." Like that unrepentant, hardened son depicted in Deuteronomy 21, Eli's sons were wicked to the core. They had done everything they could to disobey God and profane His name, and so the final words in 1 Samuel 2:25 say that "the Lord desired to put them to death." Enough was enough. It was time for Eli to act as a responsible priest and parent and publicly denounce their wickedness to the elders of the city for punishment.

But he didn't.

Failing to Develop a Spirit of Submissiveness

Since Eli refused to take a firm stand with his sons, tolerating their evil, we see God taking over their books, declaring them bankrupt, and calling in all their outstanding debts.

> "Behold, I am about to do a thing in Israel at which both ears of everyone who hears it will tingle. In that day I will carry out against Eli all that I have spoken concerning his house, from beginning to end. For I have told him that I am about to judge his house forever for the iniquity which he knew, because his sons brought a curse on themselves and he did not rebuke them." (3:11–13)

Eli's failure is summed up in five words: "He did not rebuke them." The Hebrew term for *rebuke* used here means "to cause to grow dim" or "to weaken." Eli did nothing to dim the fiery passions that burned out of control in his sons. He did nothing to weaken their rebellious wills that stood hard and fast against God. In essence, he did nothing to help develop a submissive spirit in them.

Conclusion

Eli's parental example is a tragic one, but all too common. He was a success at work—but a failure at home. Training up children costs, and the fee is counted out in the small change of minutes and hours you invest in your children. Eli didn't pay the price to train his sons, and in the end, it cost him, his sons, and all Israel dearly.[2]

2. One cost often overlooked is the example Eli set for Samuel. For further study, read how Samuel came to live with Eli (1 Sam. 1:1–2:11); how he was directly involved in conveying God's message of judgment to Eli concerning him and his sons (3:1–18); and how he ended up, unbelievably, making similar mistakes with his own sons (8:1–5).

In *Traits of a Healthy Family,* author Dolores Curran points out that Americans have traditionally judged families as good or bad based on exterior signs like affluence, church attendance, and community involvement. Accordingly, a good family . . .

> was one that was self-sufficient, didn't ask for help from others, supported its institutions, was never tainted with failure, starved before it went on welfare, and met all the criteria of good families as determined by community and church.
>
> People paid little attention to what went on inside a family—whether there was good communication, emotional support, or trusting relationships. People were only concerned about whether a family met the more obvious, visible family standards set by society.[3]

Eli was the head of a "good family." He held the top position in his field for forty years. You could imagine him as president of the Kiwanis Club in Ephraim or chairman of several prestigious boards in Shiloh. Yes sir, Eli's professional reputation was impeccable.

But then there was his parental reputation. The character of his two sons, Hophni and Phinehas, didn't exactly turn out to be impeccable. Poor Eli. Were he alive today, some would probably shake their heads and say, "I just don't understand why those two ne'er-do-well boys aren't like their father. He's such a good priest and hard worker." Success at work, however, doesn't necessarily guarantee success at home, as we have seen in Eli's life . . . and perhaps our own.

Is your family a "good family"? Do you take as many pains in your parental responsibilities as you do in your professional duties? Take a moment to evaluate the health of your home in light of Eli's mistakes.

———————◆———————

Are you preoccupied with your profession to the exclusion of your family's needs?

❑ blindly so   ❑ partially so   ❑ not at all

3. Dolores Curran, *Traits of a Healthy Family* (San Francisco, Calif.: Harper and Row, 1983), p. 7.

Are you refusing to face serious problems in your children's lifestyles?

❏ wearing blinders ❏ passively peeking ❏ eyes wide open

Are you responsive to the warnings of others regarding your kids?

❏ turn a deaf ear ❏ hear but ignore ❏ hear and heed

Do you become part of the problem by passively condoning the wrongs your children commit?

❏ partner in crime ❏ mildly disapprove ❏ act firm in love

———————◆———————

What happened to Eli can happen to any of us. God has recorded his mistake as a danger signal for us today. Is God warning you about a certain area of your family life that needs correction?[4]

Living Insights

Hophni and Phinehas might gladly have traded the privileges that came with having a high-powered father for just one experience like what happened to a teen named John.

> "The best time I have had with my dad was when burglars broke into our summer cottage at the lake. The police said we should come up to see what was missing. Well, our whole family's made the trip dozens of times, but this time there were just the two of us. It's a six hour drive. I'd never spent six hours alone with him in my whole life. Six hours up, six hours back. No car radio. We really talked. It's like we discovered each other. There's more to him than I thought. It made us friends."[5]

Did Hophni and Phinehas ever have six hours alone with Eli?

---

4. These Living Insights and the Digging Deeper are revised versions of those from the study guide *The Strong Family*, coauthored by Ken Gire, Living Insights by Lee Hough, from the Bible-teaching ministry of Charles R. Swindoll (Anaheim, Calif.: Insight for Living, 1991), pp. 97–101.

5. From an interview by Ann McCarroll, as quoted by Curran in *Traits of a Healthy Family*, p. 42.

One hour? Thirty minutes? Was Eli ever more than just Israel's high priest to them? Was he ever just their father, their friend? If the way Hophni and Phinehas behaved is any indication, it seems that the three lived separate lives under the same roof.

When was the last time you really talked—alone and uninterrupted—with one of your children?

_____

_____

_____

In what ways have you shared yourself with each of your children, rather than just sharing an activity?

_____

_____

_____

In what ways have you developed closeness with your children? Have you spent as much time and energy with them as with your friends?

_____

_____

_____

What would you share about your faith and life if you had your child's company for six uninterrupted hours?

_____

_____

_____

Many good books are available today that deal with the topic of communication. Two such books are *The Power of Modeling* by Jorie Kincaid (Colorado Springs, Colo.: NavPress, 1989); and *The Language of Love* by Gary Smalley and John Trent (Pomona, Calif.: Focus on the Family Publishing, 1988).

Digging Deeper

The contrast between Eli's leadership in the nation and in his own home is disturbing, bringing some unsettling questions to the surface: Does his failure at home tarnish or even negate the success of his ministry? Should he have been removed as priest of God's house until he had put his own house in order? In light of the condition of his family, was Eli even qualified to lead the people of Israel?

Allowing his sons to grow like untended weeds certainly gave the tendrils of failure a foothold in Eli's ministry. Yes, he served for forty years, but look at the quality and end result of his service. The people's holy offerings were defiled (1 Sam. 2:12–17); the people themselves were degraded (v. 22); Eli's sons were exalted above the Lord (v. 29); the ark of the covenant, one of the nation's most sacred possessions, was captured by an ungodly enemy (5:11–22); and even Eli's descendants were later entangled in the mass of unwieldy growth that was his life (2:30–33).

Eli's leadership of Israel was greatly marred by his lack of leadership at home. But though this is true, it does not mean that we should cast Eli's example aside as worthless.

Probably the most important thing we can take from his story is a more solid understanding of God's requirements for leadership given in 1 Timothy 3:4–5.

> He must be one who manages his own household well, keeping his children under control with all dignity (but if a man does not know how to manage his own household, how will he take care of the church of God?).

Our world is in desperate need of true leaders. Aspiring to fill this role is commendable but at the same time sobering, because leadership is a lifestyle, not just a forty-hour-per-week job. Before we appoint leaders or seek a leadership position ourselves, let's remember Eli and look first at the home. Because that's where true leadership begins.[6]

6. If you would like to do some further exploring on this issue of leadership, we would like to recommend the following books: *The Seven Habits of Highly Effective People* by Stephen R. Covey (New York, N.Y.: Simon and Schuster, 1989); *Spiritual Leadership*, rev. ed., by J. Oswald Sanders (Chicago, Ill.: Moody Press, 1980); and *Leadership: Influence That Inspires* by Charles R. Swindoll (Waco, Tex.: Word Books, 1985).

Chapter 7

TRAINING YOUR CHILD
Deuteronomy 6:1–9

How-to books seem to crowd bookstores like schoolchildren lining up for recess. Pushing and shoving to line the shelves, they elbow their way into the marketplace, promising to teach us everything from how to lose weight to how to get rich without risk in thirty days.

You'll even find the how-to crowd roughhousing over in the family section. It seems that everyone from humorists to Harvard Ph.D.s have something in print that promises to be "the" secret for raising obedient, non-spill, self-cleaning, self-actualized children.

Needless to say, the cacophony of contradictory counsel is confusing. That's why it's so helpful to turn aside to the clarion voice of our heavenly Father in the Scriptures. There we will find the essential, unchanging truths necessary for training our children.

Let's step into the Old Testament section of God's library and look up a classic child-rearing passage from the book of Deuteronomy.

Training Must Start with the Parents

While revealing His wisdom on the training of children, God reveals first Himself and then a cornerstone command upon which all parenting must stand.

> "Hear, O Israel! The Lord is our God, the Lord
> is one![1] And you shall love the Lord your God with
> all your heart and with all your soul and with all
> your might." (6:4–5)

Notice that Moses doesn't say we're to fear God or study Him or even serve Him. The command is to *love*. That's every parent's first and foremost task. Training up children begins with moms and dads learning how to love God with their whole person—heart, mind, will, and strength. One writer explains why loving God in such a manner is so vital.

---

1. The Hebrew word for *one* is *echad* and may suggest the unity of the Father, Son, and Holy Spirit within the Godhead. The same word is found in Genesis 2:24, where *one* is used of the union between Adam and Eve.

> Some love [God] with the strength of the mind and
> the weakness of the emotion—the intellectualist in
> religion; some love him with the strength of emotion
> and the weakness of the mind—the sentimentalist
> in religion; some love him with the strength of the
> will and the weakness of emotion—the man of iron
> who is not very approachable. But loving God with
> the strength of the mind, the strength of the emo-
> tion, and the strength of the will—that makes the
> truly Christian and truly balanced and the truly
> strong character.[2]

The apostle Paul possessed that kind of strong character, and
he passed it on to his followers as a father would to his children.

> The things you have learned and received and heard
> and seen in me, practice these things; and the God
> of peace shall be with you. (Phil. 4:9)

The basic truth so clearly demonstrated by Paul, for all parents
to remember, is that nothing can happen through us until it has
happened to us. We cannot give what we do not have. We cannot
train up our children to love God with all their heart, soul, and
might if we do not love God with all of ours. It's not enough to
just send them to Sunday school. In fact, it's not even close. Real
parenting, the kind God wants accomplished in the home, hinges
on the reality of the parents' own love for the Lord. If it's not there,
whatever instruction we give our children will likely come off as a
noisy gong or clanging cymbal (see 1 Cor. 13:1). And the longer
and louder we bang out our sermons, the more our children will
probably just cover their ears.

Training Children Is the Responsibility of Parents

Knowing and loving the Lord establishes the basis for effective
parenting, but our task doesn't stop there. Parents must build on
that solid foundation by following this next guideline.

> "And these words, which I am commanding you
> today, shall be on your heart. And you shall teach

---

2. E. Stanley Jones, as quoted by Gordon MacDonald in *Ordering Your Private World,* exp.
ed. (Nashville, Tenn.: Oliver Nelson, Thomas Nelson Publishers, 1985), p. 94.

them diligently to your sons and shall talk of them when you sit in your house and when you walk by the way and when you lie down and when you rise up." (Deut. 6:6–7)

This verse is loaded with practical wisdom. First, we have the command—"and you shall teach them diligently to your sons." The words *teach diligently* are a translation of the Hebrew word *shanan*, meaning "to sharpen." It is a vivid word conveying the idea of the parents' teaching penetrating the children, piercing through to give them a sharp edge for living, making them keen, perceptive, and discerning.

Second, we're told the process—"and you shall talk." Please take note of this. It doesn't say we should preach, moralize, lecture, or dogmatically demand this or that. It simply says *talk*. How? In a natural, normal, unforced, and unstructured way, like you would if you were talking about sports or your plans for the day.

If the only time we mention God is in formal sessions using felt boards and lesson plans, our children won't grasp how a loving God can be a natural part of everyday living. Instead, they'll grow up with a compartmentalized view of life. God will be restricted to church, revivals, Bible studies; and the rest of life—school, business, the arts, science, politics, you name it—will be totally separate.

But Moses is saying, "Don't divide life into sacred and secular segments. Love God in and through *all* that you do." And that involves communicating Him to your children in the ordinary settings mentioned in the last half of the verse.

- *When you sit in your house.* One of the most natural times for a family to sit together in the home is at mealtime. It is a wonderful opportunity for spontaneous sharing, listening, and learning about the Lord. Now, some well-meaning parents try to force God into the family circle with words like, "OK, everybody, listen up. After dessert, we're going to share religious thoughts. Suzie, you'll go first." But it doesn't work that way. That kind of forced "talking" is stilted and unnatural. Instead, why not give a recent example of how God has worked in your own life? Or share something humorous like a mistake you've made. Kids love stories like that. It makes it easier for them to relate to you and for you to relate how God is working in your life.

- *When you walk by the way.* When is the last time you took a walk with one of your children or went driving with no specific destination—just to get away and talk? That's training. That's normal, nonstructured time when children often feel the freedom to unload what's on their minds. Perhaps you have to drive a child to school or ballet lessons or soccer practice. Why not turn off the radio and talk instead? Take advantage of these kinds of teachable moments.

- *When you lie down.* Have you discovered the value of bedtime? Instead of sending a child off to bed, why not crawl in bed beside him? Snuggle up in the soft glow of the night-light and listen. Children settle down as sleep slowly takes hold, and often they will bring up the joys, fears, hopes, and hurts they feel. Even wrongs are more readily admitted in the secure comfort of that moment. Many wonderful, poignant, even funny moments await the parent who is willing to make that extra effort to listen at bedtime.

- *When you rise up.* Some people wake up each morning like a bear coming out of a long winter sleep—grouchy, snarling, and ready to bite. If you grew up with a parent like that, you know how destructive that can be to a child's spirit. Early mornings are so important—they can shape a child's whole day. Parents, don't miss out on the opportunity you have each day to send your children out to play or to school with a powerful reminder of Jesus' loving presence through a hug, a helping hand, or a warm, encouraging smile.

Training Must Prepare Children for Life Away from Home

The third and final guideline from our passage for parents to remember is this: The training we give our children should prepare them for the real world as "children of God above reproach in the midst of a crooked and perverse generation" (Phil. 2:15b). To accomplish that goal, we must teach them to keep God's commands in their minds.

> "And you shall bind them as a sign on your hand and
> they shall be as frontals on your forehead." (Deut. 6:8)

Some Jews over the centuries have taken this passage literally and wear small leather boxes containing portions of Scripture, known as phylacteries, around their foreheads and left forearm (see

Matt. 23:5). But Moses' words are meant to reach far deeper than adorning ourselves with Scripture. The hand symbolizes our work, what we do for a living. And the forehead represents the mind, our thought life, our philosophy of living. God's Word is to be inseparably bound up in all that we do and think. Remember, Mom and Dad, during those early formative years that are so crucial in your child's life, you are the only Bible they will know. What they read in your actions and words is what they will believe about the Lord. Is your version an accurate translation of Him?

Last, in Deuteronomy 6:9, Moses gives one more figurative illustration that will help us prepare our children for life away from home.

> "And you shall write them on the doorposts of your
> house and on your gates."

Here again the meaning of Moses' words goes beyond the literal. The doorposts and gates signify all our domestic and community activities. Every action of our lives, those lived inside the home as well as out, is to have His Word etched in it.

Conclusion

Training children is not simply a matter of doing the right things; it is being the right kind of person. It's not about technique; it's about who and what we are. Do you really love the Lord, Mom? Dad, have you bound God's Word to everything you do and think? If so, then your children will learn of loving God from you. They will see and experience how the Scriptures can be a lamp to their feet and a light to their path in all of life, not just in a building we call church (see Ps. 119:105).

Without a genuine love for God and an intimate knowledge of His Word, all the techniques in the world will not help you train up your children according to God's guidelines. Remember, we cannot give what we do not have. So ask yourself, Is it a love for Him I'm giving my children—or simply a list of do's and don'ts?

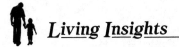 *Living Insights*   STUDY ONE

Dinner Saturday night:
"Dear Lord, we thank Thee for Thy bountiful blessings of which we are about to partake. Amen."

Breakfast Sunday morning:

"You'll go to church if I say you'll go to church—and you're going to church!"

Here endeth the spiritual training in many homes. Well . . . some parents do a little more than this. For instance, the father who binds the biblical principle of discipline to his hand:

"Hey, HEY, H E Y ! Knock it off before I come in there and start bustin' some fannies."

Sure, no problem . . . kids naturally understand that this means they're loved and should work out their differences according to Philippians 2:1–8 and Romans 12:16–21. Wouldn't you?

No? Well then, what about that family Bible the family never reads? Just its presence in the home must surely have a profound impact on helping children integrate God's commands into daily living. Right?

Forgive me for being facetious, but I think you get the point. Training children to love the Lord and obey His commands takes more than forced church attendance, heavy-handed discipline, and a neatly displayed family Bible. It takes parents who genuinely love the Lord and who are willing to demonstrate that love in the way they act toward their children.

Mom and Dad, are you doing that? Can your children see Jesus in you? Do they hear His Word in your words? Will His compassion and patience be communicated by the touch of your hands and the tone of your voice? Don't tell them about Jesus, give them Jesus. Let them see by your example that God's law is perfect, restoring the soul;

> The testimony of the Lord is sure, making wise
>   the simple.
> The precepts of the Lord are right, rejoicing the
>   heart;
> The commandment of the Lord is pure, enlighten-
>   ing the eyes.
> The fear of the Lord is clean, enduring forever;
> The judgments of the Lord are true; they are righ-
>   teous altogether.
> They are more desirable than gold, yes, than
>   much fine gold;
> Sweeter also than honey and the drippings of the
>   honeycomb.

Moreover, by them Thy servant is warned;
In keeping them there is great reward.
(Ps. 19:7–11)

Parents, *you* are God's lesson plan for training up children, not Sunday schools or youth ministries or even Christian preschools. Sure, they can help, but they cannot take the place of the position and influence God has given you.

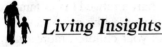

Living Insights

According to Deuteronomy 6:4–9, we're to teach our children God's Word when we sit in our homes, when we walk by the way, when we lie down, and when we rise up. To do this, obviously, we must first gain an intimate knowledge and understanding of God's Word for ourselves. In what ways, Mom and Dad, are you accomplishing this now? Use the space provided to write your answer.

_____

_____

_____

_____

Are there some avenues of biblical input that need cultivating, such as memorization, meditation, or how to conduct a Bible study of your own?

_____

_____

_____

If you need help in any of these areas, we recommend contacting the Navigators at 1-800-366-7788 or your local Christian bookstore. Both have excellent resources to help you grow as a student of the Word.

Chapter 8

THE HOME TRAINING
OF JESUS
Luke 2:39–52

It seems the older we get as parents, the more dear memories become. Each of the photographs lovingly arranged in our family albums is framed with nostalgia. And, if you're like most parents, you probably treasure the early photos of your children more than any others. Also, like most parents, you probably wish you had taken more pictures during that time.

So far in our studies, we've looked primarily at our own family albums. We've been studying principles to help us fill those pages with snapshots that are vibrant, colorful, and sharply focused on God's Word. In this study, however, we're going to browse through a family album on the coffee table of Mary and Joseph, the parents of the only perfect child—Jesus.

From Infancy to Twelve Years of Age

We'll be looking at two photographs of Jesus as a boy—one of His childhood (Luke 2:39–40) and one as He stands on the threshold of His teenage years (vv. 51–52). Neither are detailed portraits, but enough of an image is present to give resolution to those early, formative years. If you pick up the first snapshot and look carefully, you'll recognize some defining features.

> And when [Mary and Joseph] had performed everything according to the Law of the Lord, they returned to Galilee, to their own city of Nazareth. And the Child continued to grow and become strong, increasing in wisdom; and the grace of God was upon Him. (vv. 39–40)

Working quietly in the background are two committed parents—committed to the Lord and committed to their child. And their commitment is meticulous, "[performing] everything according to the Law of the Lord." What a fortunate setting for young Jesus to grow up in.

Physical Growth

As we focus on "the Child," the first detail that catches our attention is His physical stature—"and the Child continued to grow and become strong." The casualness of that statement suggests a very normal pattern of growth. You don't get the impression that Mary and Joseph tried to hurry Jesus for His debut in society with a lot of nagging and prodding. Obviously, He was a uniquely gifted young man, yet He was allowed to develop at His own pace. Written between the lines is a normal process of calm, consistent, unhurried development.

Mental Growth

Just as Jesus grew physically, He also developed mentally and emotionally—revealed in the words "increasing in wisdom" (v. 40). Literally, the phrase means "He continued to be filled with wisdom," the tense suggesting a process of continued action.

The apostle Paul, writing from prison decades later, describes how this process worked in his young friend Timothy's life. First, he mentions in 2 Timothy 3:13 the conditions of the world in which they lived: "evil men and impostors will proceed from bad to worse, deceiving and being deceived." So, in verses 14–15, he exhorts Timothy to be on the alert by continuing to follow the process that began in his home.

> You, however, continue in the things you have learned and become convinced of, knowing from whom you have learned them; and that from childhood you have known the sacred writings which are able to give you the wisdom that leads to salvation through faith which is in Christ Jesus.

The first thing we observe is *the importance of childhood training*. Back in chapter 1, the door to Timothy's home stands ajar, and we are given a peek at his childhood influences: "I am mindful of the sincere faith within you, which first dwelt in your grandmother Lois, and your mother Eunice" (v. 5). What a heritage! In the relay of truth in Timothy's line, no one dropped the baton.

Another truth we see in both Timothy's and Jesus' early lives is *childhood training is a process* (3:14–15). Receiving knowledge regarding the Scriptures was Timothy's first tottering step toward spiritual maturity. The second, firmer step in the process was learning, or appropriating, the knowledge imparted to him. The confident third step was the development of personal conviction. Finally, he learned to walk in wisdom, which is the skill of applying biblical principles to everyday life. Essentially, it is looking at life from God's point of view.

And, like Timothy, Jesus continued to increase His wisdom as He grew older.

Spiritual Growth

Back in Luke 2:40, as Jesus increased in stature and in wisdom, "the grace of God was upon Him." This means that as His life began to unfold under Mary's and Joseph's committed guidance, grace descended upon Him as naturally as dew upon a morning flower. Spiritual life seems to have a delicate timing mechanism ticking away in the seeds of our children's souls. In its own season—when the ground is fertile—germination will take place; and when the angle of the sun is right, the grace of God will bring that bud to full flower. It doesn't take a parent's pulling on the petals or fertilizing it to death. Growth is as much a process in the spiritual realm as it is in the physical (see Mark 4:26–28). We can plant seeds and water them, but ultimately, it is God who causes the growth (see 1 Cor. 3:6).

From Adolescence to Thirty Years of Age

Turning from Jesus' childhood years, we next see Him as a young man. After the incident in the temple (Luke 2:41–50), we know nothing more of His early years.

His Subjection to His Parents

As we stare at this second snapshot of Mary, Joseph, and Jesus all returning from Jerusalem, something incongruous catches our eye.

And He went down with them, and came to Nazareth;
and He continued in subjection to them; and His
mother treasured all these things in her heart. (v. 51)

Our eyes hesitate over the word *subjection*. The Greek word is a military term that means "to fall in rank under the authority of another." With that in mind, look again at the picture. To one side of the photograph we see Mary and Joseph walking on the road to Nazareth. Walking with them and under their authority is the young

Jesus. It's a study in contrasts: Perfect child—imperfect parents. Creator—creatures. King of Kings—subjects of the King. Yet, in spite of the apparent miscasting, He submits to their authority. And suddenly the picture becomes an insightful example for all young people to follow.

Children are to cooperate with their parents' rules without griping. They should relinquish their stubbornness when there is a conflict at home, responding to their parents' counsel and correction with appreciation and genuine humility. Also, they should fulfill their responsibilities with a good attitude.

Jesus knew what it was like to have imperfect, limited parents. But He treated them with respect anyway. And in doing so, He gave Mary something to treasure in her heart.

His Development

The last verse in Luke 2 reads, "And Jesus kept increasing in wisdom and stature, and in favor with God and men." The picture resembles the one in verse 40; but if you compare the two closely, you will find that wisdom and physical development have changed places. Wisdom is now in the foreground overshadowing stature. The Greek word translated *increasing* indicates more vigorous movement and adds another dimension to the picture. Jesus, as a teenager, continued to grow, but His wisdom was vigorously outdistancing His physical development.

The final description regarding His development, "in favor with God and men," pictures Jesus as balanced. He was not so spiritual that He was out of touch with the world around Him; nor was He submerged in society's system to the point that He had no spiritual distinctives. Both His vertical and His horizontal relationships were in harmony and in balance.

Learning Obedience through Suffering

As we close the album, we see the words from Hebrews 5:8 engraved in gold lettering on the cover:

Although He was a Son, He learned obedience from the things which He suffered.

The pictures we have seen thus far show a growing boy living out His childhood in favor with God and men. However, the pictures to be developed later in Jesus' life were ones of persecution, betrayal, trials, and crucifixion—of pain and suffering. Most parents seem intent on sparing their children from all forms of suffering; they intercede or intervene whenever pain threatens to touch them. This protectiveness is natural, but it should be held in balance with the reality that many of the important lessons of life are learned through pain and suffering.

Living Insights STUDY ONE

Let me introduce you to three children whose childhoods aren't anything like Jesus' unhurried upbringing.

◆

"Davey, put your dinosaurs down and come over here; Daddy has something important to tell you. Now I want you to be a big boy and listen very carefully. Mommy has . . . uh, well, she's decided to go on a long trip."

"Will she be home before I go to bed?"

"No, Davey, she won't."

"Why not?"

"Well, I'm afraid she's not ever coming back."

"How many days is that, Daddy?"

◆

It was a party like any other: ice cream and cake, a donkey poster and twelve haphazard tails, and a door prize for everyone including Toby, the birthday girl's little brother who couldn't do anything but smear icing.

"Ooh," sighed seven-year-old Melissa as she opened her first present. It was Calvin Klein jeans. "Aah," she gasped as the second box revealed a bright new top from Gloria Vanderbilt. There were Christian Dior undies from grandma—a satiny little chemise and matching bloomer bottoms—and mother herself had fallen for a marvelous party outfit from Yves St. Laurent. Melissa's best friend gave her an Izod sports shirt, complete with alligator emblem. Added to that a couple of books were, indeed, very nice and predictable—except for the fancy doll one guest's eccentric mother insisted on bringing.[1]

———————◆———————

Janet is ten years old but has many adult responsibilities. In addition to taking care of her clothes and room, she must prepare breakfast for herself and her younger sister and make sure that they get off to school on time. (Her mother leaves for work an hour before Janet needs to get to school). When she gets home, she has to do some housecleaning, defrost some meat for dinner, and make sure her sister is all right. When her mother gets home Janet listens patiently to her mother's description of the "creeps" at work who never leave her alone and who are always making cracks or passes. After Janet helps prepare dinner, her mother says, "Honey, will you do the dishes? I'm just too tired," and Janet barely has time to do some homework.[2]

———————◆———————

Davey, Melissa, and Janet—all three share the common malady of having to grow up too fast. In his book *The Hurried Child*, author David Elkind writes,

> Hurried children are forced to take on the physical, psychological, and social trappings of adulthood before they are prepared to deal with them. We dress our children in miniature adult costumes (often with designer labels), we expose them to gratuitous sex and violence, and we expect them to cope with an increasingly bewildering social environment—divorce, single parenthood, homosexuality. . . .
> The pressure to grow up fast, to achieve early in the area of sports, academics, and social interaction, is very great in middle-class America. There is no room today for the "late bloomers.". . . Children have to achieve success early or they are regarded as losers.[3]

1. Susan Ferraro, "Hotsy Totsy," *American Way Magazine*, April, 1981, p. 61. As quoted by David Elkind in *The Hurried Child: Growing Up Too Fast Too Soon* (Reading, Mass.: Addison-Wesley Publishing Co., 1981), p. 8.

2. Elkind, *The Hurried Child*, p. 149.

3. Elkind, *The Hurried Child*, pp. xii, 17.

Mom and Dad, are you pressuring your children to grow up fast? Are you pushing your son to be a peewee Babe Ruth? Are you driving your preschool daughter to start earning a college-of-her-choice GPA? Perhaps you're not hurrying them, but be aware that the media will, with a shameless exploitation that borders on criminal.

"Hurry up and worry about how you look; hurry up and worry about your weight; hurry up and be the best in sports; hurry up and wear only designer clothes; hurry up and fix your hair like an adult; hurry up and buy this toothpaste to be sexually hip; hurry up and talk like an adult; hurry up and be exposed to graphic violence, profanity, and immorality" . . . and on it goes.

Children stand little chance in today's world of not having their childhood taken from them if their parents don't recognize the danger and actively guard that precious possession. Mom and Dad, how can you protect your son or daughter from being exposed to too much too soon?

_____

_____

_____

_____

_____

_____

_____

_____

_____

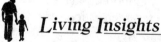 **Living Insights** STUDY TWO

We can't always protect our children from being hurried to grow up. Situations occur that force them to deal with things they're not yet ready to handle—but must. As parents, what can we do to help them?

David Elkind offers this invaluable insight. From his studies of the hurried child, he discovered

> an almost universal assumption on the part of adults regarding young children: We tend to assume that children are much more like us in their thoughts than they are in their feelings. But in fact, just the reverse is true: *children are most like us in their feelings and least like us in their thoughts.*[4]

Take, for example, Elkind's story of little two-year-old Will. His father developed a cerebral hemorrhage that left him retarded and helpless. The mother and son went for counseling and here is her description of what happened.

> "Will stopped playing and stared. Then all at once, he started picking up toys and throwing them around the room viciously, as hard as he could. I thought, 'Oh God, what am I doing here?' I had had a perfectly happy little boy. Then my little Will ran over and started hitting me. I was mortified. I was furious at the counselor, but before I could speak, she had calmly knelt next to Will and was quietly explaining that it was okay to throw toys because they were only toys; and while he certainly didn't have a right to hit his mother, he certainly had a right to be mad at her.
> "'Mom didn't take care of everything, did she, Will?' the counselor asked.
> "'No,' said Will with feeling, 'she didn't. She let my daddy get sick and I hate her.' Carefully and at length the counselor explained that even doctors had no way to keep Daddy from getting sick and neither did Mommy . . . then Will climbed into [my] lap, clung to [me] and sobbed." "I was astonished," Will's mother concluded, "I never dreamed that two-year-olds have such deep feelings."[5]

Blaming his mother for not taking care of everything obviously

4. Elkind, *The Hurried Child*, p. 187.

5. Janet Marks, "Crises Intervention for Children: A Psychological Stitch in Time," *Town & Country*, October, 1980, as quoted by Elkind, *The Hurried Child*, pp. 187–88.

wasn't a rational response on Will's part. But, of course, a two-year-old can hardly be expected to deal with such a tragedy on that level. What he can do is feel, deeply, as that unsuspecting mother discovered. And that's where we as parents can help our children cope with being hurried. Remember Elkind's insight—children are most like us in their feelings, not their thoughts.

> Accordingly, when we have to hurry young children, when they have to be at a day-care center or with a baby-sitter, we need to appreciate children's feelings about the matter. Giving children a rational explanation, "I have to work so we can eat, buy clothes, and so on," helps but it isn't enough to deal with the child's implicit thought—"If they really love me, they wouldn't go off and leave me." We need to respond to a child's feeling more than to his or her intellect. One might say, for instance: "I'm really going to miss you today and wish you could be with me." The exact words are less important than the message that the separation is painful but necessary for you too. And it is equally important, when you pick your child up at the end of the day, to say something about how happy you are to see him or her. By responding to the young child's feelings, we lessen some of the stress of hurrying.[6]

If hurrying has been unavoidable in your child's life, how can you begin to lessen the stress of it?

_____

_____

_____

_____

What central messages need communicating that might help them deal with these pressures emotionally?

_____

_____

6. Elkind, The Hurried Child, p. 188.

70

Chapter 9

SEEDS A MOTHER PLANTS

2 Timothy 1:1–7

She cooks, she cleans, she comforts, she corrects. She has six pairs of hands and eyes in the back of her head. *Mother.*

For some, this word conjures up images of June Cleaver, complete with lace apron and pearls—singing lullabies, baking brownies, kissing away a child's hot tears. Others envision the Erma Bombeck model, who drives a wood-paneled station wagon and whose hobby is dust. Whatever the type, no one has more influence than a mother. For better or worse, she will forever impact the life of her child.

Tough and tender, wise and warm, a mother must be all things to all her family . . . at all times. That's quite a job description, and anyone who is a mother or has watched one in action knows there's no career more demanding or more endangered in today's society. In this lesson, let's look closely at several key qualities, scattered like seeds throughout 2 Timothy 1:1–7, that these special women plant in the lives of their children.

The Background of 2 Timothy

The apostle Paul penned this epistle to his coworker and close friend, Timothy, while shackled in a dank Roman dungeon near the end of his life. Yet it is here, in this living coffin for the condemned, that Paul wrote one of his warmest, most personal letters.

The opening verses reveal Paul's close relationship with Timothy and set a nostalgic tone for the rest of the letter.

> Paul, an apostle of Christ Jesus by the will of God, according to the promise of life in Christ Jesus, to Timothy, my beloved son: Grace, mercy and peace from God the Father and Christ Jesus our Lord.
>
> I thank God, whom I serve with a clear conscience the way my forefathers did, as I constantly remember you in my prayers night and day. (1:1–3)

We know from Acts 16:1 that Timothy had a Jewish mother and a Greek father. So when Paul addresses him here as his "beloved son," he's referring to their spiritual kinship. For Paul had personally discipled Timothy and they had traveled extensively together as missionaries. So special was this relationship that, even in his last days, Paul remembered Timothy in his prayers "night and day."

Seeds Planted by Timothy's Mother

In the verses that follow, we'll discover the qualities that drew the Apostle to forge a fifteen-year friendship with this devout young man, qualities Timothy learned from his mother.

Transparent Tenderness

Paul first mentions Timothy's tears.

> Even as I recall your tears, so that I may be filled with joy. (2 Tim. 1:4b)

Paul remembers Timothy's tenderness, a trait that's cultivated by example rather than precept. And most often, it is the mother's example that encourages tenderness in a child.

For generations, American boys have been raised to believe that men don't cry, that they should be tough, not tender. Toughness and tenderness have mistakenly been seen as mutually exclusive qualities. And yet, two of history's "manliest" men, David and Jesus, displayed moments of great tenderness.

David wept openly with Jonathan in 1 Samuel 20:41 and repeatedly throughout the Psalms. The Psalms also show that same tenderness in David's sensitivity to the Lord. Jesus, too, wept over the death of his friend Lazarus (John 11:35) and over the unrepentant city of Jerusalem (Luke 19:41). He tenderly sat children on His lap, touched untouchable lepers, and compassionately fed hungry followers.

Mom, don't lose that quality of tenderness—it's one of your greatest contributions to your daughter as well as your son. Your warm embrace, eager smile, and soft reply will be a safe harbor for the child who's tossed and battered by life's stormy seas.

Authentic Christianity

A second seed Timothy's mother planted was genuine faith.

> For I am mindful of the sincere faith within you, which first dwelt in your grandmother Lois, and your mother Eunice, and I am sure that it is in you as well. (2 Tim. 1:5)

72

The Greek term for *sincere* is *anupokritos*, which means "un-hypocritical." His faith had an authentic quality to it—a quality first modeled for him by Grandma Lois and then by his mother, Eunice. Paul goes on to exhort young Timothy to continue in the faith he learned in his childhood.

> You, however, continue in the things you have learned and become convinced of, knowing from whom you have learned them; and that from child-hood you have known the sacred writings which are able to give you the wisdom that leads to salvation through faith which is in Christ Jesus. (3:14–15)

In our fast-food, hurry-up world, people want authentic faith instantly. But the genuine faith Timothy demonstrated didn't spring up overnight. It was cultivated over the years—at home.

In *Celebration of Discipline*, Richard Foster writes:

> Superficiality is the curse of our age. The doc-trine of instant satisfaction is a primary spiritual problem. The desperate need today is not for a greater number of intelligent people, or gifted people, but for deep people.[1]

Authentic faith or artificial fruit—which are we cultivating in our homes? Fake fruit may be pleasing to the eye, but it lacks the taste and nourishment of real fruit, as well as the seeds necessary to reproduce itself. Artificial fruit may be produced overnight, but authentic faith, deep faith, is homegrown over a lifetime.

Inner Confidence

The third seed relates to Timothy's self-esteem.

> And for this reason I remind you to kindle afresh the gift of God which is in you through the laying on of my hands. For God has not given us a spirit of ti-midity, but of power and love and discipline. (1:6–7)

Paul reminds this probably-somewhat-intimidated new pastor of two very important things. Namely, that the gift he has is "of

---

1. Richard J. Foster, *Celebration of Discipline* (San Francisco, Calif.: Harper and Row, Pub-lishers, 1978), p. 1.

God" and that God has given him not "a spirit of timidity, but of power and love and discipline." Here Paul helps Timothy overcome his shyness and regain his inner confidence by appealing to his strengths.

Now, the text is clear that Timothy's spiritual gift came through Paul's ministry (v. 6), but the authentic faith of his home cultivated the soil in which that gift flourished (see 3:15). God gives power, and He gives it very effectively through our roots. He builds confidence through the impact of our parents.

A primary way to build confidence in children is to equip them with strengths they can draw from in times of weakness. Obviously, at the time Paul wrote, Timothy was going through a period of withdrawal as a result of something he feared (1:6–7). Instead of focusing on the negative and criticizing him, however, Paul gives him positive encouragement based on certain strengths Timothy already had within him.

Demonstrative Love

Look again at verse 7a:

> For God has not given us a spirit of timidity, but of
> power and *love*. . . . (emphasis added)

The Greek term Paul uses for love is *agapē*, which means "unselfishness." It pictures a demonstrative love that seeks the highest good of another person. And where is that type of love learned? Where does a child usually first see *agapē* love in the flesh? In a mother who gets up, without complaint, at all hours of the night to comfort a sick child . . . in a mother who continuously cooks and cleans so another may be fed and refreshed . . . in a mother who goes the extra mile past boredom to read for the hundredth time the child's favorite story with first-time enthusiasm. No one wears the fabric of selfless love quite as naturally and as elegantly as a mother.

In another letter, this time to the Corinthians, Paul devoted an entire chapter to the subject of unselfish love (1 Cor. 13). One woman has written a paraphrase that aptly describes this essential ingredient of mothering.

> If I talk to my children about what is right and
> what is wrong, but have not love, I am like a ringing
> doorbell or pots banging in the kitchen. And though

I know what stages they will go through, and understand their growing pains, and can answer all their questions about life, and believe myself to be a devoted mother, but have not love, I am nothing.

If I give up the fulfillment of a career to make my children's lives better, and stay up all night sewing costumes or baking cookies on short notice, but grumble about lack of sleep, I have not love and accomplish nothing.

A loving mother is patient with her children's immaturity and kind even when they are not; a loving mother is not jealous of their youth nor does she hold it over their heads whenever she has sacrificed for them. A loving mother does not push her children into doing things her way. She is not irritable, when the chicken pox have kept her confined with three whining children for two weeks, and does not resent the child who brought the affliction home in the first place.

A loving mother is not relieved when her disagreeable child finally disobeys her directly and she can punish him, but rather rejoices with him when he is being more cooperative. A loving mother bears much of the responsibility for her children; she believes in them; she hopes in each one's individual ability to stand out as a light in a dark world; she endures every backache and heartache to accomplish that.

A loving mother never really dies. As for home-baked bread, it will be consumed and forgotten; as for spotless floors, they will soon gather dust and heelmarks. And as for children, well, right now toys, friends, and food are all-important to them. But when they grow up it will have been how their mother loved them that will determine how they love others. In that way she will live on.

So care, training, and a loving mother reside in a home, these three, but the greatest of these is a loving mother.[2]

2. Dianne Lorang, as quoted in *Keep the Fire Glowing*, by Pat Williams, Jill Williams, and Jerry Jenkins (Old Tappan, N.J.: Fleming H. Revell Co., 1986), pp. 152–53.

Self-control

Take a final look at 2 Timothy 1:7, this time noting the closing word.

> For God has not given us a spirit of timidity, but of power and love and *discipline.* (emphasis added)

Self-discipline, also referred to as self-control, is the ability to say no when the majority says yes, or to say yes when everyone else is saying no—an increasingly rare trait today.

Moms, balance your tenderness and love with discipline. Set parameters, teach your children self-control, and know when it's time to say, "That's it; that's far enough."

In his excellent book *Hide or Seek,* James Dobson tells the story of a research project conducted by Dr. Stanley Coopersmith, associate professor of psychology at the University of California. After studying 1,738 middle-class boys and their families over a number of years, Coopersmith identified three important differences between the families of boys with high self-esteem and those with low self-worth.

First, *the high-esteem children were more loved and appreciated at home.* Their parents' love was deep and real; their words had substance.

Second, and perhaps most revealing, *the high-esteem group had parents whose approach to discipline was significantly more strict.* They taught self-control. In contrast, the parents of the low-esteem group were much more permissive, creating a sense of insecurity. These boys were more likely to feel that no one cared enough to enforce the rules.

Third, *the high-esteem group had homes characterized by democracy and open communication.* Once boundaries had been established, the boys had the freedom to ask questions and express themselves in an environment of acceptance.[3]

Mom, don't underestimate the value of teaching self-control. In your discipline, you are building your children's character, enhancing their self-esteem, and helping them learn to be responsible for themselves.

---

3. See James Dobson, *Hide or Seek,* rev. ed. (Old Tappan, N.J.: Fleming H. Revell Co., 1979), pp. 92–93.

Conclusion

A mother's heart is the schoolroom where the child learns the ABCs of life—where tenderness is translated into all its subtle nuances, where faith is multiplied, where confidence is read aloud, where love is conjugated into all its tenses, and where self-discipline stands as monitor. This is why it is said that "one good mother is worth a hundred school masters."[4]

Living Insights   STUDY ONE

Remember the times in your childhood when your mom planted the seeds of transparent tenderness?

I remember the times when I was sick. Mom would untie my Buster Browns and gently coax me to the couch. Then the ritual began that I'll never forget: pillows fluffed up and carefully positioned, a comfortable quilt snugly wrapped, a cool washcloth, and the thing I remember best—the tender touch of Mom's hand. Just the warm press of her slender hand on my forehead reassured me that everything would be all right. It spoke the healing truths that I was loved, that I belonged, that somebody cared if I was sick— someone bigger, who understood how to call forth the curative powers of mysterious medicines and ancient home remedies. All that in a touch, a tender, healing hand.

Now, when my energetic three-and-a-half-year-old gets sick, I remember to fluff the pillows, to wrap him snugly in a quilt, and to bring him a cool washcloth. But most of all, I remember to lay my hand on him. It's your hand, Mom; you taught me that. The tenderness, assurance, and comfort he feels was put there by you.

What has your mom taught you? Let's find out in the next Living Insight.

Living Insights   STUDY TWO

Can you recall a specific way your mother modeled transparent tenderness? Or what about authentic Christianity, inner confidence,

---

4. George Herbert, as quoted in *Speaker's Encyclopedia of Stories, Quotations, and Anecdotes,* ed. Jacob M. Braude (Englewood Cliffs, N.J.: Prentice-Hall, 1955), p. 266.

demonstrative love, or self-control? Was it in the way she calmed domestic storms, showed mercy, fed multitudes of your friends with only a loaf of bread and a box of fish sticks, healed the sick, felt compassion for the lost, the downtrodden, or the weak?

Write down what you recall as if you were telling it to someone, because we're going to ask you to do just that after you finish.

_____

_____

_____

_____

_____

Children love to hear about when their mommies and daddies were little. So why not tell them, for example, how their grandmother sowed a seed of transparent tenderness in your life when you were a child? Then encourage them to talk about those times when they sense that same tenderness coming from you or perhaps how you can do a better job of sowing that seed in their lives.

One last thing. If possible, thank your mom for the godly seeds she planted in you. You can never pay her back, but you can bring her great joy by letting her see how those seeds are blossoming in your life.

Chapter 10

MASCULINE MODEL OF LEADERSHIP
Selected Scriptures

In his book *Promises to Peter,* Charlie Shedd tells how the title of his message on parenting changed with his experience of fatherhood. In his early years on the speaking circuit, before he was a father, he called it "How to Raise Your Children." People came in droves to hear it. Then Charlie had a child, and it was a while before he gave that message again. When he did, it had a new name: "Some Suggestions to Parents." Two more children and a number of years later, he was calling it "Feeble Hints to Fellow Strugglers." Several years and children later, he seldom gave that talk. But when he did, his theme was "Anyone here got a few words of wisdom?"

It's tough being a dad. It's almost impossible to live up to your own standards, to say nothing of God's. And the toughest thing of all is facing the fact that you are leaving an indelible thumbprint on the life of each of your children. Whether you're nuts-and-bolts practical or you scrape the Milky Way with visionary ideas; whether you're strong and aggressive or weak and passive; whether you're a workaholic or an alcoholic—there's not a dad who doesn't leave his fingerprints all over his children as he molds and shapes them into the adults they will become.

How can fathers do this carefully and wisely? In this lesson we will take a few tips on parenting from the apostle Paul. We don't know if Paul was ever a father in the literal sense; but in his first letter to the Thessalonians, we see some fatherly characteristics that are well worth emulating.

A Little Background

When Paul took a trip to Thessalonica, he saw potential in that city and wanted to stay, even though he was pursued and persecuted

This lesson and the following Living Insights are adapted from the chapter "Masculine Model of Leadership," in the study guide *The Strong Family,* coauthored by Ken Gire, Living Insights by Lee Hough, from the Bible-teaching ministry of Charles R. Swindoll (Anaheim, Calif.: Insight for Living, 1991).

(see 1 Thess. 2:1–2). So for six weeks, he poured himself into that handful of believers, working night and day to establish them in their newborn faith. And although he was never to return for another in-depth visit, the Thessalonian Christians had captured his heart.

When he later heard about the waves of persecution that threatened to drown their belief, he threw them two life preservers: his trusted friend Timothy (3:2) and a heartfelt letter of encouragement. Streaming through his pen was the love of a father's heart.

> But we proved to be gentle among you, as a nursing mother tenderly cares for her own children . . . imploring each one of you as a father would his own children. (2:7, 11b)

Five Traits of a Good Father

"As a . . . mother . . . as a father"—these words appear nowhere else in Paul's writings. And it's from this context of Paul's fatherly heart that we draw some principles for parenting.

A Fond Affection

The first quality Paul illustrates is affection:

> Having thus a fond affection for you. (v. 8a)

He had at his fingertips half-a-dozen Greek terms he could have used, but Paul picked a word for *affection* found only this once in all the New Testament—a word that means "to feel oneself drawn to something or someone." It's a term of endearment taken from the nursery—a term both masculine and tender . . . the picture of a father gently cradling his tiny child.[1]

How often, though, do we really express this kind of "fond affection"? It's easy to hug and kiss a baby, even a small child. But as that child grows up, physical affection is often replaced with physical aloofness. Gordon MacDonald, in his book *The Effective Father*, includes a chapter called "Please Show Me That You Care." In it he writes:

> The physical expression of our approval is of

---

1. This same affection is demonstrated by the father when his prodigal son returns. "And he got up and came to his father. But while he was still a long way off, his father saw him, and felt compassion for him, and ran and embraced him, and kissed him" (Luke 15:20).

great importance. We affirm what a person is, and we appreciate what a person does. But this assurance must be given in more than words. *Affection*, the non-verbal communication of closeness, touching, and stroking is among the most important experiences we share with one another.[2]

Research shows that sexual promiscuity in a woman can often be traced to a lack of fatherly affection in her childhood and adolescence.[3] So fathers, demonstrate your love—now, before your child starts looking for it in the wrong ways in the wrong places.

A Transparent Life

The second half of verse 8 goes on to illustrate the second guideline: a transparent life.

> We were well-pleased to impart to you *not only the gospel of God but also our own lives*, because you had become very dear to us. (emphasis added)

Isn't the gospel important? Absolutely! And isn't it enough? Absolutely not!

It's essential that your children hear the gospel if they are to come to know the Savior you love; and it's even better if the Good News comes from your own lips. But they need more than that. They need instruction about life, and they need a father who lets them watch him live it, mistakes and all. They need to see how you handle your finances, how you make decisions, what your values are, and what makes you laugh. They need to hear you admit when you're wrong and see you stand up for what's right. They need to know you inside out—and to feel your interest and belief in them. The word *impart* means "to convey, to contribute, to share fully" . . . with children who know without a doubt they are "very dear" to you.

An Unselfish Diligence

The third trait is found in verse 9, where Paul draws a picture of hard work, of a dad applying himself to the task at hand.

---

2. Gordon MacDonald, *The Effective Father* (Wheaton, Ill.: Tyndale House Publishers, Living Books, 1977), p. 229.

3. Dan Benson, *The Total Man* (Wheaton, Ill.: Tyndale House Publishers, 1977), p. 178.

81

For you recall, brethren, our labor and hardship, how working night and day so as not to be a burden to any of you, we proclaimed to you the gospel of God.

To the Thessalonians, Paul's life was a picture of hard work—"labor and hardship"; diligent work—"working night and day"; and unselfish work—"so as not to be a burden to any of you."

This is a detailed sketch of financial responsibility and bearing up under the strain of demands. What an example for your children to see! What they need to see is their dad doing a day's work for a day's pay; and they need opportunities to earn their own way.

A Spiritual Authenticity

Verses 9b–10 sketch the lines of two important aspects of a father's spiritual responsibility: belief and behavior.

We proclaimed to you the gospel of God. You are witnesses, and so is God, how devoutly and uprightly and blamelessly we behaved toward you believers.

Unlike Paul, many fathers leave the spiritual aspect of child raising to Mom. But the truth is, dads need to teach Christ too, and then live their lives in a way that backs it up.

Paul's spiritual authenticity did just that. He behaved "devoutly," "uprightly," and "blamelessly." The word *devoutly* highlights "religious piety" and describes a person devoted to God's service.[4] The Greek term for *uprightly* has a slightly different shade of meaning. Fundamentally, it refers to "conformity to God's law."[5] So what is in view here is Paul's moral conduct. The final description of his behavior—*blamelessly*—reveals the degree of his devotion to God and the degree of morality in his conduct. Both are without spot or blame. And all of these characteristics add up to spiritual authenticity.

A Positive Influence

The final trait in this study for fathers to emulate is a positive influence.

4. Robert L. Thomas, "1 Thessalonians," *The Expositor's Bible Commentary* (Grand Rapids, Mich.: Zondervan Publishing House, Regency Reference Library, 1978), vol. 11, p. 255.

5. Leon Morris, *The First and Second Epistles to the Thessalonians* (Grand Rapids, Mich.: William B. Eerdmans Publishing Co., 1959), p. 83.

Just as you know how we were exhorting and encouraging and imploring each one of you as a father would his own children, so that you may walk in a manner worthy of the God who calls you into His own kingdom and glory. (vv. 11–12)

A good father exerts a positive influence on his children. He exhorts. He encourages. He implores. These are the words Paul uses to describe how a father relates to his children. He doesn't shout. He doesn't demean. He doesn't dictate. He is not a demagogue—he is their dad.

Dan Benson, in his book *The Total Man*, tells us the results of a disturbing survey: for every single positive statement made in the average home, there are ten negative ones.[6] It's not easy to be positive and at the same time constantly correct children as they mature. But children whose ears are full of the words "No" and "Don't" and "Stop that!" learn not to trust their instincts, not to try. Children who hear "That's great!" and "You can do it!" as often as they hear "That's not a good idea" will face new challenges with self-confidence and explore their potential without fear.

Dads, "be quick to hear, slow to speak and slow to anger" (James 1:19). Choose your words, your tone of voice carefully. Be conscious of the fact that "death and life are in the power of the tongue" (Prov. 18:21a), and before you speak, ask yourself:

- Are my words stimulating? Challenging?
- Are they encouraging? Hopeful?
- Are they instructive? Helpful?

Oh, and one more thing. Watch out for "Dadisms." What's a "Dadism," you say? It's a species of speech peculiar to fatherhood and generally hated by all kids. Newswriter Mark Patinkin explains it best in a hilariously convicting article titled "'You're Grounded'—and Other Dadisms."

There's a . . . book out filled with 80 pages of the one-liners your mother used to tell you. It's called *Momilies*. You'd probably recognize most of it. For example:

6. Benson, *The Total Man*, p. 183.

83

"Sit up straight."

"Don't cross your eyes or they'll freeze that way."

"If you can't say anything nice, don't say anything at all."

It got me thinking about the things fathers used to say. They usually carried a different tone. What follows are a few Dadisms:

- I will break every bone in your head.
- I will break every bone in your body.
- Because I'm your father, that's why. . . .
- When I was a boy . . .
- . . . I used to walk eight miles to school every morning . . .
- . . . after finishing my chores. . . .
- You want your allowance, you know where the mower is.
- How'd you like to spend the rest of the summer in your room? . . .
- You call that hair combed?
- Talk to your mother.
- Is that any way to talk to your mother?
- She bore you in pain.
- You want something to cry about? I'll give you something to cry about. . . .
- Douglas, I mean Hugh, I mean Matthew . . . whatever your name is . . . come here.
- Now.[7]

Recognize any of these? You're grounded.

Just kidding. But remember, all the exhorting, encouraging, and imploring have one unified, lofty purpose: so that you may train your children to "walk in a manner worthy of the God who calls [them] into His own kingdom and glory" (1 Thess. 2:12).

7. Mark Patinkin, "'You're Grounded'—and Other Dadisms," *Fort Worth Star-Telegram,* October 13, 1985, p. 6C.

In his book *Making Sense Out of Suffering*, author Peter Kreeft writes:

> I shall never forget reading about the boy in the bubble. . . . He had a rare disease (how common rare diseases seem to be!) that necessitated his living his whole life in a sterile plastic bubble. Any touch, a single germ, could kill him. All communication, recreation, education, everything was through the bubble. Finally, he was dying. Since he was doomed anyway, he asked to touch his father's hand—his father, who had loved him and stayed with him all his life. What unspeakable love and pain was in that one touch![8]

Many children feel like that boy—their whole childhood is spent trapped inside a sterile family bubble void of any physical affection. They, too, ache for the approving touch of their father's hand.

In *How to Really Love Your Child*, Dr. Ross Campbell emphasizes that giving our children physical affection is crucial. For example, young boys up to age seven or eight need to be held and hugged. Then,

> as a boy grows and becomes older, his need for physical affection such as hugging and kissing lessens but his need for physical contact does not. Instead of primarily "ooey-gooey love stuff," he now wants "boy-style" physical contact such as playful wrestling, jostling, backslapping, playful hitting or boxing, bearhugs, "give-me-five." . . . These ways of making physical contact with a boy are just as genuine a means of giving attention as hugging and kissing. Don't forget that a child *never* outgrows his need for *both* types.[9]

8. Peter Kreeft, *Making Sense Out of Suffering* (Ann Arbor, Mich.: Servant Books, 1986), p. 5.

9. D. Ross Campbell, *How to Really Love Your Child* (Wheaton, Ill.: Scripture Press Publications, Victor Books, 1977), pp. 47–48.

As for girls and their needs, Campbell writes:

> A father helps his daughter to approve of herself by showing her that he himself approves of her. He does this by applying . . . unconditional love, eye contact, and physical contact, as well as focused attention. A daughter's need for her father to do this begins as early as two years of age. This need, although important at younger ages, becomes greater as the girl grows older and approaches that almost magic age of thirteen.[10]

Dads, the chances are good that many of you had fathers who were culturally conditioned not to show any physical affection. Instead of receiving an affirming hug when you felt rejected or hurt as a child, you were probably told, "Little boys don't cry" or, "Be a man, gut it up."

Don't make that same mistake with your children. Don't just tell them you love them or assume that they know this simply because you buy them things. Show them. Imitate your Father in heaven who demonstrated His love for you through Christ (see Rom. 5:8; Eph. 2:4–7).

Living Insights STUDY TWO

Appropriate physical touching is not all that's required of a good father. He must also learn how to exhort and encourage his children with the touch of his words.

Are your words heavy-handed or gentle? Calloused or sensitive? Irritable or encouraging?

> *How many times do I have to tell you?* . . . *You never get it right.* . . . *Why can't you be like your brother?* . . . *Shut up!*

> Death and life are in the power of the tongue.
> (Prov. 18:21a)

> *Get down.* . . . *Leave that alone.* . . . *Go away—stop—quit—DON'T!* . . . *Because I say so!*

---

10. Campbell, *How to Really Love Your Child*, p. 51.

A soothing tongue is a tree of life,
But perversion in it crushes the spirit.
(15:4)

I love you. . . . I'll help you. . . . How was your day? . . .
Mom and I thank God for you. . . . I'm sorry. . . . You did a great
job cleaning up your room. . . . Thank you. . . . Please. . . .
You go first. . . . I used to fall off my bike a lot too! . . . Your
attitude has been really good today.

Pleasant words are a honeycomb,
Sweet to the soul and healing to the bones.
(16:24)

With your spouse's help, list the encouraging phrases you say
most often in routine exchanges at home.

_____

_____

What are some of the hurtful words that need to be weeded out
from your family conversations?

_____

_____

Don't use bad language. Say only what is good and
helpful to those you are talking to, and what will
give them a blessing. (Eph. 4:29 LB)

Why not make it a family project to print or paint this verse
on poster board or newsprint, discuss what it means, have everyone
commit to doing it, and then hang it someplace where it will be a
visible reminder to all?

Living Insights

In his poignant book *The Gift of Remembrance*, author Ken Gire
reminisces about the life-changing pictures his father left to him in
a scrapbook of memories. Pull up a chair and listen as Ken describes
a sensitive snapshot that captures what it means to live a transparent
life, to impart our lives as fathers to our children.

I remember a third picture.

One Saturday when Dad was home—
    often he wasn't because he worked so much—
    I answered a knock on the door.

A handicapped boy,
    seventeenish,
    stood on the other side of the screen,
    selling socks.
    He introduced himself
    and went straight into his sales pitch.

His face contorted as he talked,
    most of the words coming out sideways-
    sounding.
    A flushed mingling of fear and sorrow
    came over me.
    With an awkward politeness I excused myself
    to get Dad.

He invited the boy in.
    I sat on the living room chair and just watched.
    The boy opened his briefcase, revealing
    an assortment of what I thought looked
    like "old-men's" socks. You know, the sheer,
    see-through kind that nobody wears
    anymore—except old men.

I didn't know much about money back then,
    other than how much you could get for cashing
    in
    Coke bottles littered along the roadside.
    All I knew was, we never seemed to have any.
    And what little we had never stretched far
    enough
    to cover the end of the month.
    So I listened
    to see how my dad would send the boy away.

But he didn't send him away.
    He listened to him with patience,
    spoke to him with kindness,
    treated him with respect.

He examined the socks,
and, to my round-eyed surprise,
bought three pairs of those frightful things.
Black, brown, and navy, if I remember right.

The boy shook my dad's hand and said good-bye.
Then he shook mine,
smiled,
and stuttered something.
I nodded as if I understood
and smiled back. . . .

Dad never sat me down and told me,
    "Son, this is how you treat someone
    less fortunate than yourself,
    someone who's disabled or disadvantaged."
    He never told me that; he simply showed me—
    but with the purity of never knowing he did.

I found that when I wrote my first book,
    it was about a mentally disabled boy.
    When I did volunteer work,
    it was with the handicapped.
    And every time I encounter those who are
    in some way bent or broken,
    my heart softens.
    I send up a little prayer—
    that the load they carry
    may be made easier to bear,
    that they may be protected
    from the cruelties of this world,
    and that they may experience as much
    as they can of the goodness
    life has to offer.

And one more thing,
    I smile.[11]

11. Ken Gire, *The Gift of Remembrance* (Grand Rapids, Mich.: Zondervan Publishing House, 1990), pp. 17, 19, 23.

Chapter 11

YOU AND YOUR DAUGHTER
(PART ONE)
Selected Proverbs

*G*one with the Wind, Margaret Mitchell's first and only novel, stands as a classic, both as a book and as a film. The backdrop to the story is the war-torn American South. But it's not so much a story about the Civil War. It's more a story about one woman— Scarlett O'Hara—a beguiling charmer whom men hovered over like bees on a blossom. However, under the coy twirl of the parasol that shaded her fine-china skin, beneath her rose-petal lips, behind the flirtatious flutter of her inviting eyes hid a heart of "snares and nets" (Eccles. 7:26).

For contrast, the author placed Scarlett beside the kind, selfless, tender Melanie. Next to her, Scarlett is seen for what she really is—a self-centered, manipulative, even ruthless woman.

In similar style, Proverbs often compares and contrasts its characters. We will compare and contrast two sets of women and, in doing so, learn about the qualities that can help our daughters become godly women.

The Foolish Woman versus the Wise Woman

Consider the two women in Proverbs 14:1.

> The wise woman builds her house,
> But the foolish tears it down with her own hands.

Let's examine each detail of the negative example first.

The Foolish Woman

Literally, the Hebrew word for foolish means "dull, thick, sluggish." The foolish woman is dulled to wisdom, calloused to correction, and sluggish in her response to God. Destruction lies in the wake of most every wave she makes.

The next phrase, *tears down*, means "to destroy," and it tells us something about this woman. She destroys her home and the people in it, dismantling them look by look, conversation by conversation, relationship by relationship until nothing is left. The tragic guilt of her actions is underscored by the emphatic phrase *with her own hands*. In the end, after years of troubling her own house, she will only "inherit wind" (11:29a).

No parents want a future like that for their little girl. But what many moms and dads fail to understand is that the foolish woman of Proverbs 14 started out as a foolish daughter—a daughter whose destructive bents were never fully recognized or effectively dealt with. So let's look at four diagnostic X rays of a foolish woman from Proverbs. Perhaps they will help us determine whether the condition exists in our daughters and what we can do to stop the malignancy before it spreads.

(1) *She is boisterous.* Notice the first sign in 9:13.

The woman of folly is boisterous,
She is naive, and knows nothing.

By *boisterous*, the text doesn't mean energetic or playful. Rather, the thought is one of commotion, rowdiness, and turbulence. Picture an electric mixer whirling batter all over the kitchen, and you get something of the idea.

The chaos in her life is related to her being *naive*, a quality we sometimes equate with innocence and therefore admire. However, where innocence keeps one free and wholesome, naiveté leaves a girl open to danger through her lack of discernment and sound, informed judgment. Her thinking lacks the clarity to grasp the meaning of a situation and make a constructive choice; her heart lacks the depth of understanding that would lead her turbulent soul toward a more peaceful path.

(2) *She makes a mockery of sin.* Proverbs 14:9a states: "Fools mock at sin." The foolish woman of chapter 9 illustrates this as she makes light of adultery.

"Stolen water is sweet;
And bread eaten in secret is pleasant."
(v. 17)

Her conscience is insensitive to sin, causing her to be flippant about morals and recklessly self-indulgent. Right and wrong are not important to her, only what is sweet and pleasant. Her live-for-the-moment lifestyle is short-sighted, obscuring the long-term effects of her actions.

(3) *She is deceptive.* Proverbs 14:8b tells us that "the folly of fools is deceit." A foolish woman can look you eyeball-to-eyeball

91

and, without batting a lash, deceive you in the most convincing way. The distinction between true and false vanishes into whatever is most convenient, and truth loses its meaning for her.

(4) *She is quarrelsome.* A final feature of foolishness appears in Proverbs 20:3.

> Keeping away from strife is an honor for a man,
> But any fool will quarrel.

The Hebrew term translated *quarrel* means "to burst forth in a rage, a tantrum," which shows us that a foolish daughter would be argumentative and given to angry outbursts.

Now that you know what the symptoms of foolishness are, put your daughter behind the X-ray machine and take a good, hard look. Is she in a constant state of turbulence, uneasy and agitated? Is sin "no big deal" to her, a joke? Is she deceitful and given to frequent lying? Does she look for a fight and try to start trouble?

If you see these symptoms in your daughter, the prognosis for her future is not good. In fact, we may say with a surgeon's frankness, her home will be like Scarlett's—troubled, torn down, and literally gone with the wind.

Equally bleak is the future of the foolish child's parents.

> He who begets a fool does so to his sorrow,
> And the father of a fool has no joy.
> (17:21)

Those parents, however, who detect foolishness in their daughter early and deal with it decisively will grace the world with a Melanie—a wise woman who builds up her home.

But how exactly can parents help their children rid themselves of this deadly foolishness? Only one proverb actually describes the procedure:

> Foolishness is bound up in the heart of a child;
> The rod of discipline will remove it far from him.
> (22:15)

Coddling a child who is dull and insensitive, thick in his or her conscience, and who makes a mockery of guilt and sin is a waste of time. Only consistent discipline applied with a physician's unflinching firmness and compassion will, as the proverb states, remove foolishness from the heart of a child. With his usual helpfulness, Dr. James Dobson gives parents practical advice on how to do this.

The overall objective during the preadolescent period is to teach the child that his actions have inevitable consequences. One of the most serious casualties in a permissive society is the failure to connect those two factors, behavior and consequences. Too often, a three-year-old child screams insults at his mother, but Mom stands blinking her eyes in confusion. A first grader launches an attack on his teacher, but the school makes allowances for his age and takes no action. A ten-year-old is caught stealing candy in a store, but is released to the recognizance of his parents. A fifteen-year-old sneaks the keys to the family car, but his father pays the fine when he is arrested. . . . You see, all through childhood, loving parents seem determined to intervene between behavior and consequences, breaking the connection and preventing the valuable learning that could have occurred. . . .

How does one connect behavior with consequences? By being willing to let the child experience a reasonable amount of pain or inconvenience when he behaves irresponsibly. When Jack misses the school bus through his own dawdling, let him walk a mile or two and enter school in midmorning (unless safety factors prevent this). If Janie carelessly loses her lunch money, let her skip a meal. Obviously, it is possible to carry this principle too far, being harsh and inflexible with an immature child. But the best approach is to expect boys and girls to carry the responsibility that is appropriate for their age, and occasionally to taste the bitter fruit that irresponsibility bears.[1]

The Wise Woman

In contrast to the foolish woman, "the wise woman builds her house" (14:1a). She's constructive instead of destructive. She establishes and maintains a strong, solid home.

---

1. James Dobson, *Dr. Dobson Answers Your Questions* (Wheaton, Ill.: Tyndale House Publishers, 1982), pp. 232–33.

So how do parents raise their daughters to be such wise women? Proverbs 31 gives us five areas on which to concentrate.

First, *help her realize the value of being wise.*

> An excellent wife, who can find?
> For her worth is far above jewels. . . .
> She opens her mouth in wisdom,
> And the teaching of kindness is on her tongue.
> (vv. 10, 26)

When your daughter recognizes that wisdom is more precious than jewels (see 3:13–18), she will have taken the first step toward gaining that wisdom.

Second, *develop in her a caring spirit.* A wise woman has a servant's heart, investing herself in building up others.

> She rises also while it is still night,
> And gives food to her household,
> And portions to her maidens. . . .
> She extends her hand to the poor;
> And she stretches out her hands to the needy.
> (vv. 15, 20)

Your daughter is more likely to develop a sensitive, giving spirit if she sees the spirit of Christ incarnate in your everyday life (compare Mark 10:45; Phil. 2:3–8).

Third, *cultivate the skills of her hands.* This is the tangible expression of wisdom that helps her support and provide for herself.

> She looks for wool and flax,
> And works with her hands in delight.
> (Prov. 31:13)

Practical skills will serve her well throughout life as they foster her confidence and equip her to adeptly manage life's many responsibilities.

Fourth, *teach her how to handle money.*

> She considers a field and buys it;
> From her earnings she plants a vineyard. . . .
> She makes linen garments and sells them,
> And supplies belts to the tradesmen.
> (vv. 16, 24)

Girls need sound financial wisdom just as much as boys do. By opening up the world of money—teaching her to save, balance a checkbook, budget, avoid debt, invest, provide for retirement—you put in place priceless safeguards for your daughter's well-being. Ignorance and dependent helplessness in this area will not be the beauty marks of femininity; they will become the bruises of a person taken advantage of.[2]

Fifth, *open her eyes to the blessings of hard work*. A wise woman knows how to diligently apply herself to a task.

> She girds herself with strength,
> And makes her arms strong. . . .
> She stretches out her hands to the distaff,
> And her hands grasp the spindle.
> (vv. 17, 19)

And she will be rewarded by her efforts throughout her life:

> Strength and dignity are her clothing,
> And she smiles at the future. (v. 25)

Now that's what you want for your daughter, isn't it? By applying these five principles to your parenting, you will see your daughter develop strength and dignity . . . and a future to smile at.

The Contentious Woman versus the Gracious Woman

Another contrasting set of women in Proverbs is the contentious and the gracious woman. As before, let's examine the negative example first. Stand back and gaze at the disturbing portrait painted by the following verses from Proverbs.

The Contentious Woman

> The contentions of a wife are a constant dripping.
> (19:13b)

> It is better to live in a corner of a roof,
> Than in a house shared with a contentious woman.
> (21:9)

> It is better to live in a desert land,
> Than with a contentious and vexing woman.
> (v. 19)

2. An excellent resource for teaching your children how to handle money is *Money Matters for Parents and Their Kids*, by Ron and Judy Blue (Nashville, Tenn.: Thomas Nelson Publishers, 1988).

> A constant dripping on a day of steady rain
> And a contentious woman are alike;
> He who would restrain her restrains the wind,
> And grasps oil with his right hand.
> (27:15–16)

Several images stand out in this picture. First, a leaky faucet. If you've ever had one keep you awake at night, you understand. Second, the corner of a roof. If you've ever been on your roof to fix an antenna, you know things would have to be pretty bad to consider living there. Third, a desert with blistering, relentless sun—doesn't sound too inviting, does it? Fourth, constant dripping on a rainy day, eroding your spirit drop by drop. And fifth, slippery oil. Try grabbing ahold of it sometime; it's frustratingly impossible.

All these images picture a woman given to strife. She thrives on stirring up conflict and unhappiness. And she always manages to get in the last word, the last jab. Like a continual drip . . . drip . . . drip, she drives you to the limits of your patience and sanity.

What causes a daughter to behave like this? An unchecked, stubborn will. Unless parents start early and work hard to develop a gracious, humble, teachable will in their daughter, Proverbs warns that "calamity will come suddenly; instantly [s]he will be broken, and there will be no healing" (6:15).[3]

Fortunately, God gives us another picture to go by—the woman of Proverbs 11: "A gracious woman attains honor" (v. 16a).

The Gracious Woman

To be gracious means "to show favor." It is a picture of the person who is accepting and appreciative, thoughtful and considerate. This characteristic is most commonly used in reference to God:

> The Lord is compassionate and gracious,
> Slow to anger and abounding in lovingkindness.
> (Ps. 103:8)

Mirror graciousness to your daughter, clearly and consistently, and glimpse by glimpse she will become a changed person. Her words, appearance, and attitude will reflect the grace she sees in

---

3. The story of Jezebel's death in 2 Kings 9:29–37 is an excellent example of this proverb.

you. And someday, that daughter will grow to attain honor as a gracious woman.[4]

Living Insights

Now that we have compared and contrasted the wise woman and the foolish in Proverbs, let's compare and contrast the wise and foolish *influences* in our daughters' lives.

One of the primary influences is TV. James Dobson writes:

> By the time the average preschool child reaches fourteen years of age, he will have witnessed 18,000 murders on TV, and countless hours of related violence. . . . Dr. Saul Kapel states, furthermore, that the most time-consuming activity in the life of a child is neither school nor family interaction. It is television, absorbing 14,000 valuable hours during the course of childhood! That is equivalent to sitting before the tube eight hours a day, continuously for 4.9 years!
>
> . . . I am also concerned about the current fashion whereby each program director is compelled to include all the avant-garde ideas. . . . In recent seasons, for example, we were offered hilariously funny episodes involving abortion, divorce, extramarital relationships, rape, and the ever-popular theme, "Father is an idiot."[5]

According to an article in *Time* magazine, the average viewer sees more than 9,000 scenes of suggested sexual intercourse or innuendo on prime-time TV in one year.[6]

Another major influence is advertising. Because teens spend and influence family spending to the tune of well over 150 billion dollars a year, the business and entertainment communities have

---

4. For additional help in teaching your daughter this Christlike characteristic, spend some time in the company of the Bible's wise and gracious women: Ruth, Hannah, Abigail, Esther, Mary (mother of Jesus), and Mary (Martha's sister).

5. Dobson, *Dr. Dobson Answers Your Questions*, p. 457.

6. Claudia Wallis, Cathy Booth, Melissa Ludtke, and Elizabeth Taylor, "Children Having Children," *Time*, December 9, 1985, p. 81.

tailored their advertising to exploit adolescent needs. In particular, they focus on the average teen's problem with self-esteem. By the time your daughter graduates from high school, she will have been bombarded by almost one million commercials telling her that she is something less than complete without a particular product.

But more than just products are being sold. Advertisers are selling images. Images of the rich and beautiful, sexy and popular, strong and powerful. And needy teenagers are buying. *Time* magazine noted, "Our young people . . . don't even buy toothpaste to clean their teeth. They buy it to be sexually attractive."[7] Influence? You bet.

What about the movie industry? According to Robert Coles, Harvard child psychologist and author of *The Moral Life of Children*, the values in today's movies are "hedonism, sexuality, violence, greed, selfishness."[8]

And what about music? "Violence, the occult, sadomasochism, rebellion, drug abuse, promiscuity, and homosexuality are constant themes," says *U.S. News and World Report*. Couple this with the fact that teens "listen to an estimated 10,500 hours of rock music between the seventh and 12th grades alone—just 500 hours less than the total time they spend in school over 12 years" and, well, you get the picture.[9]

Then, of course, there's the influence of peer pressure, MTV, magazines, pop stars, and the list goes on. Children are being swept away in a society that, like the fool in Psalm 14:1, believes that "there is no God."[10]

Now these things have not been mentioned so that everyone will burn their TV sets and stereos and go hide in the mountains. Rather, it's to give you just a sampling of the powerful influences

7. Wallis, Booth, Ludtke, and Taylor, "Children Having Children," p. 81.

8. As quoted by Steve Huntley and Harold R. Kennedy in "Expert Advice: Keep Control of Family Fun," *U.S. News and World Report*, October 28, 1985, p. 54. For further study, read Michael Medved's *Hollywood vs. America: Popular Culture and the War on Traditional Values* (New York, N.Y.: HarperCollins Publishers, Zondervan, 1992).

9. "What Entertainers Are Doing to Your Kids," *U.S. News and World Report*, October 28, 1985, p. 46. For a more recent example of music and its influence, read George Will's article "America's Slide into the Sewer" in *Newsweek*, July 30, 1990, about the rap group 2 Live Crew.

10. See Focus on the Family's excellent video "A Generation at Risk," by Robert DeMoss, Jr., and their books *Children at Risk: The Battle for the Hearts and Minds of Our Children*, by James Dobson and Gary L. Bauer, and *When Love Is Not Enough* by Steve Arterburn and Jim Burns.

toward foolishness your daughter must contend with daily.

Take time now to think about the *wise* influences your daughter is exposed to and list them in the space provided. For example, a Bible study; volunteer work; one-on-one time with Mom or Dad discussing current issues, films, or events from a Christian perspective; music or books with godly themes . . .

_____

_____

_____

_____

_____

Last, if you do nothing to change the wise and foolish influences in your daughter's life right now, do you think she will grow to be a wise woman . . . or a foolish one?

Living Insights   STUDY TWO

Read Proverbs 31:10–31 and note all the ways this woman exemplifies wisdom and grace.

_____

_____

_____

_____

We know these traits don't just naturally occur in children; they have to be planted and watered by the parents. What do you think the parents of the woman in Proverbs 31 did to cultivate these kinds of traits in her?

_____

_____

_____

_____

_____

Of the things you listed, which are you doing for your daughter?

_____

_____

_____

_____

What, if anything, is lacking that you could focus on more? How?

_____

_____

_____

Chapter 12

YOU AND YOUR DAUGHTER
(PART TWO)
Selected Proverbs

In a fine essay titled "What Is a Girl?" Alan Beck tenderly captures the joy our daughters can bring to our lives.

> Little girls are the nicest things that happen to people. . . .
> A girl is Innocence playing in the mud, Beauty standing on its head, and Motherhood dragging a doll by the foot. . . .
> God borrows from many creatures to make a girl. He uses the song of the bird, the squeal of a pig, the stubbornness of the mule, the antics of a monkey, the spryness of a grasshopper, the curiosity of a cat, the speed of a gazelle, the slyness of a fox, the softness of a kitten. . . .
> . . . She is the loudest when you are thinking, the prettiest when she has provoked you, the busiest at bedtime, the quietest when you want to show her off, and the most flirtatious when she absolutely must not get the best of you again.
> Who else can cause you more grief, joy, irritation, satisfaction, embarrassment and genuine delight than this combination of Eve, Salome, and Florence Nightingale?[1]

Some of you are smiling and nodding in agreement; raising daughters has been a delight, the nicest thing to happen to you. Others, however, feel the dull stabs of heartache as you read these words; for you, raising a daughter has been a disaster. How the experience turns out for us depends largely upon the qualities we

---

This lesson is adapted from "You and Your Daughter (Part Two)" from the study guide *Growing Wise in Family Life*, coauthored by Ken Gire, from the Bible-teaching ministry of Charles R. Swindoll (Fullerton, Calif.: Insight for Living, 1988).

1. Alan Beck, as quoted by Dale Evans Rogers in *Time Out, Ladies!* (Westwood, N.J.: Fleming H. Revell Co., 1966), pp. 55–56.

are able to build into our daughters' lives. To continue the theme of our previous lesson, let's contrast two more pairs of women to find out which qualities need cultivating and which need culling in our daughters.

The Sensual Woman versus the Virtuous Woman

As before, let's begin our study of the opposites we find in Proverbs by examining the negative example first.

The Sensual Woman

Proverbs 2:16 describes the sexually promiscuous woman as *the strange woman*, which would be better rendered as "the estranged woman," because she is estranged from her family and alienated from the circle of proper relationships. How can you detect signs of such a woman in your daughter? Proverbs provides us five distinctive traits.

1. By her words. Proverbs 2:16 states that the sensual woman "flatters with her words," and 5:3 augments this picture:

> For the lips of an adulteress drip honey,
> And smoother than oil is her speech.

The daughter who is on her way to a life of promiscuity and ultimate emptiness depends on her ability to flatter and entice men instead of relating to them from the heart.

2. By her friends. Notice our next clue in Proverbs 2:17a—she "leaves the companion of her youth." When a daughter reaches her teens and suddenly breaks off her relationships with longtime friends, the wise parent is alerted to trouble. This is especially true if the daughter leaves her peer group and begins to run with an older, faster crowd (see also 13:20; 22:24–25).

3. By her lack of spiritual commitment. She "forgets the covenant of her God," according to 2:17b. This shows up in the daughter who forsakes the spiritual truths she once held to embrace a worldly lifestyle.

4. By her appearance. Proverbs 7:10 says she dresses "as a harlot." In the Jewish culture of that day, prostitutes dressed in a fashion that made them easily identifiable. In our day, that can be tough to distinguish from just being fashionable. Some clues include how revealing the clothing is, whether it's designed to entice others rather than to simply be attractive, and whether it does more to

express the physical than to convey the personality. Keep in touch with what's currently in style so you can really know this difference and avoid misjudging your daughter.

5. By her attitude. Proverbs 7:11–13a reveal her moods and behavior:

> She is boisterous and rebellious;
> Her feet do not remain at home;
> She is now in the streets, now in the squares,
> And lurks by every corner.
> So she seizes [a man] and kisses him.

In our last chapter, we saw the turbulence whirling through the description *boisterous*. Add to that the ideas of being disrespectful, hostile, fast, cunning, and aggressive, and the description of an immoral, destructive woman's attitude is fleshed out.

Your daughter may never run off into the treacherous terrain of a sexually promiscuous life. However, she may be wandering precariously close to its borders if you can see some of the qualities emerging in her which are reflected in the sensual woman of Proverbs.

If you do see any similarities, take these warning signs to heart and plan some positive steps. Studies have long shown that a growing daughter needs warmth, affection, and communication—especially from her father—if she is going to grow up healthy and whole. She needs smiles, hugs, and constant reassurances of your love. She needs candid talks on life, on what a man looks for in a woman, and on what the Bible says about inner and outer beauty (compare 1 Pet. 3:3–4).

Fathers, you can lose your daughters by default, simply by not being there—or if there, by being silent and passive. Instead of taking a step back in rejection, take a step forward in acceptance and give her the biggest hug, the warmest smile, and the most sincere "I love you" that you possibly can. Assure her of your love often enough, and those messages will start transforming her from the inside out.

The Virtuous Woman

In stark contrast to all the ignoble qualities of the sensual woman are the excellent traits of the virtuous woman found in Proverbs 31. According to the Hebrew, *virtuous* means she is "firm, strong, efficient, able"—she conveys a sense of moral worth. Solomon also says she is rare: "An excellent wife, who can find?" (v. 10a). She is someone of great value: "her worth is far above jewels" (v. 10b). And she is at the top of God's list: "Many daughters have done nobly, But you excel them all" (v. 29).

The entire passage of Proverbs 31:10–31 holds this jewel of a woman up as the perfect role model for every growing girl. Her finely cut facets sparkle brilliantly—she is trustworthy, diligent, capable, committed to the family's well-being, prudent, generous, strong, kind, has integrity, speaks wisely, and is appreciated by her family.

As a life assignment, begin using verses 10–31 as a prayer list for your daughter. It's the best way to get a diamond in the rough out of the rough!

The Indiscreet Woman versus the Godly Woman

In this, our final comparison, we'll learn that beauty is, indeed, only skin deep.

The Indiscreet Woman

A woman without discretion is depicted in ridiculous terms.

> As a ring of gold in a swine's snout,
> So is a beautiful woman who lacks discretion.
> (Prov. 11:22)

The word *discretion* comes from the Hebrew word meaning "to taste," carrying the idea of discriminating taste (compare Ps. 34:8). It is the ability to choose between the tasteful and the tasteless, the appropriate and the inappropriate, right and wrong, good and bad. A woman lacking that ability, no matter how beautiful, becomes as repulsive as the runny snout of a pig. Her physical beauty, like the gold ring, is totally out of harmony with her inner self.

If your daughter is moving toward maturity with discretion, three things will be true. First, she will be able to perceive that which isn't obvious—she has discernment. Second, she will be able to interpret the unspoken—she can read between the lines. And third, she senses the implications of her actions and the actions of others—she knows choices have consequences, so she chooses carefully before she proceeds.

How do you instill such discretion in your daughter? By establishing biblical wisdom as the grid through which thought and behavior are filtered. God's Word is to be her—and your—frame of reference (see Ps. 119:66, 98–100). Also model discretion daily; don't wait until she's almost grown, then give her a crash course in character. Remember, too, dads, that this involves you as well as mom. Daughters need to know a man's views, struggles, thinking, and responses as well as a woman's.

The Godly Woman

In contrast to the disgusting image of the indiscreet woman is the pleasing picture of the godly woman in Proverbs 31:30.

> Charm is deceitful and beauty is vain,
> But a woman who fears the Lord, she shall be praised.

The woman who fears the Lord realizes that charm can conceal the truth of a woman's character and beauty can mask an empty life. She understands the need to cultivate an inner Christlike beauty that's eternal. For the daughter whose love for the Lord is the most obvious adornment of her life, praise will come, and she won't act indiscreetly in order to gain the attention of others.

Are we saying, then, that parents should teach their daughters to focus only on the inner person and ignore the outer one? Is dressing nicely and wearing jewelry wrong? No. The apostle Peter touches on this issue and provides some excellent advice to every young woman.

> And let not your adornment be *merely* external—braiding the hair, and wearing gold jewelry, or putting on dresses; but let it be the hidden person of the heart, with the imperishable quality of a gentle and quiet spirit, which is precious in the sight of God. (1 Pet. 3:3–4, emphasis added)

The source of genuine beauty for the Christian woman is her inner character. What she wears on the outside should be a nice complement to her inner spirit.

One of the greatest problems, however, that your daughter will face growing up today is the Madison Avenue message that physical beauty is everything for a woman. Almost every magazine, every commercial, every billboard, every movie communicates that message either explicitly or implicitly. And unless you get close enough to your daughter to model and affirm what is precious in God's sight, she may never get the true message . . . or know how truly precious she really is.

Mom and Dad, what is it that you affirm most often about your daughter? Is it her looks? Her musical ability? Her intelligence? Good manners? What about the traits of a virtuous and godly woman? When was the last time you praised your daughter for any of those?

Honestly, many of us have no answer for that last question. Such praise is really foreign to us. Sure, we take our daughters to church regularly, but then we fail to give them the continued spiritual encouragement they need at home. If only we could see how the precious blossoms of virtue and godliness wilt in our budding daughters simply for lack of nourishing praise.

Now some of you may be thinking,

> Must I brag on my child all day for every little thing [she] does? Isn't it possible to create a spoiled brat by telling [her that her] every move is wonderful?[2]

Many parents have wondered about that same question. So many, in fact, that Dr. Dobson included it in his best-seller *Dare to Discipline*. Listen to his wise response.

> Yes, inflationary praise is unwise. . . . [Your daughter] quickly catches on to your verbal game and your words then lose their meaning. It is helpful, therefore, to distinguish between the concepts of *flattery* and *praise*.
>
> Flattery is unearned. It is what Grandma says when she comes for a visit: "Oh, look at my beautiful little girl! You're getting prettier each day. I'll bet you'll have to beat the boys off with a club when you get to be a teenager!" . . . Flattery occurs when you heap compliments upon the child for something [she] does not achieve.
>
> Praise, on the other hand, is used to reinforce positive, constructive behavior. It should be highly specific rather than general. "You've been a good

2. James Dobson, *The New Dare to Discipline* (Wheaton, Ill.: Tyndale House Publishers, 1992), p. 96.

[girl] . . ." is unsatisfactory. "I like the way you kept your room clean today," is better. Parents should always watch for opportunities to offer genuine, well-deserved praise to their children, while avoiding empty flattery.[3]

Parents, nurture your daughter's godly traits with praise. To help you do this, use the following space to note the specific ways you've seen your daughter model virtue.

_____

_____

_____

Now, on a separate sheet of paper, write your daughter a letter affirming the specific traits you've listed. It will be one of the most important letters you'll ever write, especially to her.

Living Insights

This next assignment should give you some real living insights into your daughter!

Ask her to go out for a special evening with you—dinner, entertainment, the works. Be creative, and go out of your way to make it relaxed, memorable, and *fun*. No lectures. No correction. No parent-to-child talks. Nothing heavy or intimidating.

For one evening, forget you're an adult and try to get into her world. Music and movies are generally common ground with most children. Try not to pass judgment or offer any unsolicited opinions; instead, just listen and try to gain a broader understanding of your daughter.

It would be a treat for her if you shared what you were like when you were her age—how you felt about dating, your worst date, your best date, what movies and music were popular then, how you felt about growing up, how you felt about your parents, and so forth. Tailor the evening to her age and her interests.

Make it a scrapbook memory for her—and for you too—one you both will treasure for a lifetime.

3. Dobson, *The New Dare to Discipline*, p. 96.

Chapter 13

YOU AND YOUR SON

Selected Proverbs

Seven years after the end of America's bloody Civil War, Josiah Holland wrote,

> God, give us men! A time like this demands
> Strong minds, great hearts, true faith and ready
> hands;
> Men whom the lust of office does not kill;
> Men whom the spoils of office cannot buy;
> Men who possess opinions and a will;
> Men who have honor; men who will not lie.[1]

It seems that the more times change, the more they stay essentially the same. For the call of that bygone era certainly rings through our day as well.

God, give us men. Give us Noahs, to whom You can entrust Your mighty plans; give us Abrahams, who are willing to leave home and homeland to follow Your call; give us Josephs, who would rather endure prison than violate one of Your commands; give us Daniels, who would rather face a lions' den than compromise their faith. *God, give us men.*

Before God gives us men, however, He gives us boys—boys that parents are to forge into men. To equip us for that task, the Lord has provided the book of Proverbs, which is largely the advice of a father to his son.

Five Areas of Teaching

From Solomon's advice we can glean at least five areas of teaching that are essential if our sons are to grow up to be honorable men of God.

This lesson was adapted from "You and Your Son" from the study guide *Growing Wise in Family Life*, coauthored by Ken Gire, from the Bible-teaching ministry of Charles R. Swindoll (Fullerton, Calif.: Insight for Living, 1988).

1. From Josiah Gilbert Holland's "God, Give Us Men!" in *The Best Loved Poems of the American People*, comp. Hazel Felleman (Garden City, N.Y.: Garden City Publishing Co., 1936), p. 132.

Teach Him to Stand Alone

Proverbs 1:10–19 highlights the need to teach our sons the importance of having biblical convictions and being willing to stand up for them, even when that means standing alone.

> If young toughs tell you, "Come and join us"—
> turn your back on them! "We'll hide and rob and
> kill," they say. "Good or bad, we'll treat them all
> alike. And the loot we'll get! All kinds of stuff!
> Come on, throw in your lot with us; we'll split with
> you in equal shares."
> Don't do it, son! Stay far from men like that, for
> crime is their way of life, and murder is their spe-
> cialty. When a bird sees a trap being set, it stays
> away, but not these men; they trap themselves! They
> lay a booby trap for their own lives. Such is the fate
> of all who live by violence and murder. They will
> die a violent death. (LB; see also 4:14–19)

Essentially, Solomon is warning his son that if the crowd strays from God's path, then follow the path and not the crowd—even if that means following it alone. Your child's peer group exerts a relentless pressure to conform and follow the pack. So if pointing out the right path isn't enough, perhaps a change in peer groups is necessary.

> He who walks with wise men will be wise,
> But the companion of fools will suffer harm.
> (13:20)

Changing friends is a painful and difficult experience, but there are at least two things parents can do that will encourage their son to take that step on his own. First, *teach him what a good friend really is.* In light of these qualities, have him evaluate his present friend-ships. Then have him set his sights on the type of friends he would like to have. Second, *remind him of the consequences of wrong.* Psalm 73 does a good job of teaching us not to envy those who break the law but to consider the consequences of their actions.

> But as for me, my feet came close to stumbling;
> My steps had almost slipped.
> For I was envious of the arrogant,

As I saw the prosperity of the wicked. . . .
Until I came into the sanctuary of God;
Then I perceived their end.
(vv. 2–3, 17)

Since children are impressionable, showing the end result of wrong behavior is essential for them to be able to withstand the magnetic pull their peer group can exert.

Teach Him to Be Open to God's Counsel

Along with the ability to stand alone, our sons need to learn what is involved in being open to God's counsel and reproof. Proverbs 3:11–12 talks about this sensitivity to instruction.

My son, do not reject the discipline of the Lord,
Or loathe His reproof,
For whom the Lord loves He reproves,
Even as a father, the son in whom he delights.

A tender heart toward God is one of the hallmarks of true manhood. David, the great warrior who is described as being as fierce as "a bear robbed of her cubs" (2 Sam. 17:8), is also shown to be "a man after My heart, who will do all My will" (Acts 13:22).

How can we develop a sensitivity like David's in the lives of our sons? First of all, we need to teach him to respond to our counsel (compare Prov. 1:8–9; 3:1–4; 4:1–4; 7:1–3). If he treasures our counsel, then treasuring God's counsel in his adulthood will be an easy transition.

Second, we must help him see the value of other people's correction. If he learns to respect the correction of his teachers, coaches, grandparents, and friends, it won't be so difficult to respond to God's correction later on in his life.

Third, we should share the experiences of our life with him. Principles are valuable, but lessons incarnated in our own lives give our sons something firmer to hold on to, remember, and understand. Sharing our victories and defeats and what we've learned through them makes values more real.

Fourth, we've got to spend sufficient time counseling our sons. Remember, you're not molding tin soldiers for the dime store; you're forging great men for God . . . and that takes time. Your presence and availability for your son will shape his personality for the full scope of life's responsibilities.

Teach Him How to Deal with Temptation

Not surprisingly, the two areas of temptation mentioned most in Proverbs are the temptation aroused by the opposite sex and the temptation of overindulgence in food and alcohol.

Sexual temptation. With regard to sexual temptation,[2] Proverbs 5:1–5 advises:

> My son, give attention to my wisdom,
> Incline your ear to my understanding;
> That you may observe discretion,
> And your lips may reserve knowledge.
> For the lips of an adulteress drip honey,
> And smoother than oil is her speech;
> But in the end she is bitter as wormwood,
> Sharp as a two-edged sword.
> Her feet go down to death,
> Her steps lay hold of Sheol.

As parents, we must extol the Edenic beauty of intimate marital love (see Song of Sol.; Prov. 5:15–19) and explain the dangers of the forbidden fruit of sexual relationships outside of marriage (5:20–23; 6:23–35; 7:4–27). As in Eden, temptation comes from the center of the garden—our hearts (compare Matt. 5:28). Whether your son resists lust or succumbs to it is determined on the daily battlefield of his heart.

To help prepare him for this battle, we parents need to provide him with appropriate training concerning the development of his body and its normal, God-given drives; we should teach him how to detect even the slightest glimmer of immoral enticement—from outside sources or his own heart; and we should instill in him the value of staying pure until marriage.

Also, if our sons understand the depth of the meaning of sexual love; if they can successfully form healthy and emotionally intimate relationships; and if they can truly know that women are people of value made in God's image, not simply objects of pleasure—then they will have a greater chance of resisting temptation and avoiding the heartaches it holds . . . for themselves and others.

---

2. If your son is showing signs of struggling with homosexuality, we recommend the following book, which gives compassionate, biblical counsel on how you can help him: *Counseling the Homosexual*, by Michael R. Saia (Minneapolis, Minn.: Bethany House Publishers, 1988).

Temptation to excessive indulgence. Proverbs also has some pointed advice with regard to food and drink:

> Listen, my son, and be wise,
> And direct your heart in the way.
> Do not be with heavy drinkers of wine,
> Or with gluttonous eaters of meat;
> For the heavy drinker and the glutton will come
>   to poverty,
> And drowsiness will clothe a man with rags.
> (Prov. 23:19–21)

Even more graphic are verses 29–35, which are especially relevant in our day.

> Who has woe? Who has sorrow?
> Who has contentions? Who has complaining?
> Who has wounds without cause?
> Who has redness of eyes?
> Those who linger long over wine,
> Those who go to taste mixed wine.
> Do not look on the wine when it is red,
> When it sparkles in the cup,
> When it goes down smoothly;
> At the last it bites like a serpent,
> And stings like a viper.
> Your eyes will see strange things,
> And your mind will utter perverse things.
> And you will be like one who lies down in the
>   middle of the sea,
> Or like one who lies down on the top of a mast.
> "They struck me, but I did not become ill;
> They beat me, but I did not know it.
> When shall I awake?
> I will seek another drink."
> (see also 20:1)

We need to be frank with our sons about the dangers of overindulgence and the destruction which results from letting the search for pleasure dominate their lives. They need to know how easy it is to get hooked, how false the promises of lasting pleasure are, and how terribly difficult it is to free themselves from its addicting grip.

112

Teach Him How to Handle Money

Let's look at four basic areas of financial responsibility: teaching your son how to give, how to earn, how to spend, and how to save.[3]

- Giving: He should learn to honor the Lord with his income by making giving number one on his priority list (Prov. 3:9–10), especially giving to the poor (22:9).[4]

- Earning: In order to give, he must learn a skill with which he can derive an income (see Eph. 4:28; 1 Thess. 4:11; 2 Thess. 3:6–13).

- Spending: The woman in Proverbs 31 exemplifies how to wisely spend and invest money (see especially vv. 16, 24; compare Matt. 25:14–30).

- Saving: Finally, the principle of saving is best seen in Solomon's illustration of the ant who stored food in the summer so she could eat in the winter (Prov. 6:6–8).

Teach Him the Value of Hard Work

Two more passages from Proverbs underscore another important topic, the value of hard work.

> Poor is he who works with a negligent hand,
> But the hand of the diligent makes rich.
> He who gathers in summer is a son who acts
>   wisely,
> But he who sleeps in harvest is a son who acts
>   shamefully. . . .
> The soul of the sluggard craves and gets nothing,
> But the soul of the diligent is made fat.
> (Prov. 10:4–5; 13:4)

In a nutshell, hard work pays off. It is a grave mistake to give, give, give to a child without allowing him or her to experience the value and reward of hard, diligent work. Parents, give your children specific jobs to do around the home. Help them find ways of earning

---

3. An excellent resource for teaching your children how to handle money is *Money Matters for Parents and Their Kids*, by Ron and Judy Blue (Nashville, Tenn.: Oliver Nelson, Thomas Nelson Publishers, 1988).

4. God speaks very clearly and seriously about our treatment of the poor. For additional passages, see Proverbs 14:31; 17:5; 19:17; 21:13; 22:16, 22–23; 28:27; 29:7.

money and sharing in the expenses of their education in ways that will train them for when they're on their own.

Two Added Ingredients

As you teach your son to be a man of God, you'll need two additional ingredients: *constant delight* and *consistent discipline*. While your son is learning the difficult lessons of discipline, he needs to know you care and delight in him so he won't be discouraged. Remember, everyone—including a child—learns more through positive, loving encouragement than a constant cascade of corrections.

One Transitional Verse to Ponder

As we draw this study to a close, consider one more verse from Proverbs that mentions the most important son ever born.

> Who has ascended into heaven and descended?
> Who has gathered the wind in His fists?
> Who has wrapped the waters in His garment?
> Who has established all the ends of the earth?
> What is His name or His son's name?
> Surely you know!
> (30:4)

Do you know that Son's name? Perhaps not. Perhaps you weren't given the kind of training presented in this study when you were young. Perhaps you were kicked around, ignored, resented, ill-treated, even despised. Strangely enough, so was this Son. Not by His parents, though, but by the very sons and daughters He created and for whom He came to give eternal life.

That Son's name, of course, is Jesus. He came to pay the penalty for your sins so that you could be reunited with your heavenly Father. Romans 6:23 says,

> For the wages of sin is death, but the free gift of God
> is eternal life in Christ Jesus our Lord.

If you've never placed your faith in Jesus Christ, you've missed the most important Son who's ever lived. We cannot make the kind of men out of our sons that the Scriptures teach until we first come to know God's Son for ourselves. How do we do that? According to John 3:16, it's by faith.

"For God so loved the world, that He gave His only begotten Son, that whoever believes in Him should not perish, but have eternal life."

Raising a godly son begins with knowing the Son. Are you willing to begin knowing Him now?

Living Insights

If ever there was time when Josiah Holland's poem "God, Give Us Men!" was appropriate, it is now. America is in serious trouble. Lying and cheating are commonplace. Violence and crime continue to rise. Immorality abounds with ever-increasing boldness. Corruption is incredibly rampant. Our judicial and political systems are in desperate need of reform. A financial tsunami called the national debt swells larger with each day. Health care costs are out of control, more and more taxes are chewing up our hard-earned money, and then, of course, there are the problems of rising pornography, abortion, homosexuality. On and on the list goes. This isn't doomsday-prophet hysteria, folks; this is reality, and it's disturbing, to say the least.

Take a moment to read all of Holland's poem and see if you don't agree about its relevance today.

> God, give us men! A time like this demands
> Strong minds, great hearts, true faith and ready
>   hands;
>   Men whom the lust of office does not kill;
> Men whom the spoils of office cannot buy;
>   Men who possess opinions and a will;
> Men who have honor; men who will not lie;
> Men who can stand before a demagogue
>   And damn his treacherous flatteries without
>   winking!
> Tall men, sun-crowned, who live above the fog
>   In public duty and in private thinking;
> For while the rabble, with their thumb-worn
>   creeds,
>   Their large professions and their little deeds,
> Mingle in selfish strife, lo! Freedom weeps,

Wrong rules the land and waiting Justice sleeps.[5]

Men like this aren't born—they're raised by parents who teach them biblical principles. The need is great for such godly men. Will your son be one?

Below are the five areas of training from our study. Rate yourself in regard to how you're communicating these to your son, with 5 being the score for the most effectiveness.

Standing Alone

1	2	3	4	5

Being Open to God's Counsel

1	2	3	4	5

Dealing with Temptation

1	2	3	4	5

Handling Money

1	2	3	4	5

Working Hard

1	2	3	4	5

More than your words, your example—how you handle convictions, counsel, temptation, money, and work—will be your son's most convincing teacher.[6] Is there a particular area that needs your attention? What plans could you write down that might help you raise your score at least one notch?

_____

_____

_____

_____

5. Holland, "God, Give Us Men!", *Best Loved Poems*, p. 132.

6. For further study, read *The Power of Modeling* by Jorie Kincaid, (Colorado Springs, Colo.: NavPress, 1989).

Living Insights

How much do you really know about your parents' past?

What was your father like when he was a boy? What were your mother's adolescent years like? What did your parents struggle with? Did they get along with their parents?

The sad fact is, many of us cannot answer even one of these questions. Our minds are blank when it comes to talking about our parents as people who were once children themselves. Will your son draw a blank too?

Sharing with our children about the ups and downs we experienced when we were their age is a powerful parenting tool. It helps them see us as real people, not just distant authority figures. It also builds some important relational bridges, such as empathy and identification, between generations within the family. Bottom line, sharing your experiences will help your children be more open and relate to you better as you lead them through childhood and adolescence.

Why not use this study to help incorporate some personal sharing about your past? Now, we're *not* talking about those "When I was young, I used to walk five miles to school, barefoot, in the snow, both ways" kinds of stories. Save those for when the family goes fishing.

Do this instead: First, briefly share what Proverbs says about standing alone, for example. Then share how you learned about that from your parents. Or perhaps tell of a time when you didn't stand alone and what you regret about that. Rather than always hearing success stories, your children will appreciate knowing they're not the only ones in the family who have blown it in one of the five areas we've been studying. In fact, the result of sharing our shortcomings is usually that our children are more open about their own problems and about letting us know them on a deeper, more intimate level.

Spend some time reflecting on each of the five areas listed and see if they trigger any personal stories from your life or your parents' lives that you could share with your children.

Standing Alone _____

_____

Being Open to God's Counsel _____

Dealing with Temptation _____

Handling Money _____

Working Hard _____

One last thing. Try sharing these types of stories at bedtime. No parent can hold a child's attention when it's play time and friends are calling. But when a child is in bed and not quite ready to sleep, you've got a captive audience—especially if there's humor involved. Like the time I didn't resist the temptation to make fun of my brother. I ended up hog-tied with my face covered in honey. But that wasn't the worst of it. Along came Happy, a honey-loving basset hound with enough drool to drown a person . . . Want to hear the rest of that story?

Your kids will too.

Chapter 14
RELEASING YOUR CHILD
Selected Scriptures

Picture yourself in an archery tournament where each contestant is given just one arrow and one shot to prove his or her marksmanship. You've been practicing for years, and now all your training and skill hangs in the balance of this one shot.

Setting the arrow securely to the taut string, you take a cursory look toward what now seems to be a too-distant target. As you lift the bow, beads of sweat pincushion your forehead. You pull back the bowstring, slowly, inhaling as you squint down the arrow toward the target.

Suddenly, your eye catches a bent in the arrow's shaft. Then it hits you—you forgot to check the arrow! Had you examined it earlier, you might have been able to correct it. Now it's too late. Once the bow is drawn, you can't stop; the arrow must be released. Even before you let the arrow fly, you can see the crooked outcome with agonizing accuracy.

OK, relax, exhale. Put the bow down. It's just make-believe, a "what if" kind of situation. Pretty tense, though, right? Imagine, then, the anxiety many parents feel about releasing the children God has put in their quiver. Out into the world they'll fly, hopefully reaching that distant target despite all their bents. And that's not make-believe; that's real life, and it can be a very distressing experience.

In many ways, it's completely normal to have difficult moments while releasing a child. However, many parents compound the pain and botch the release because they've never learned some basic truths about how to let their children go. Hopefully, the truths in this lesson will mop a little sweat from your brow and help steady your hand for the time that moment arrives.

Why Releasing Your Child Comes Hard

As inevitably as dandelion seeds parachute off to new soil and as instinctively as young birds stretch new wings to leave their nests, so God has designed children to grow up and start new homes of their own:

> For this cause a man shall leave his father and his

mother, and shall cleave to his wife; and they shall become one flesh. (Gen. 2:24)

In spite of how natural, how inevitable, how instinctive, and how scriptural it may be, releasing children is still difficult for most parents. Let's look at some of the reasons.

Sometimes Parents Build Themselves into Their Children

Fathers and mothers alike are sometimes guilty of living their lives through their children. They build themselves into their children instead of allowing them to develop the unique identity God designed each of them to have. Perhaps something was lacking in the parent's childhood, so he or she tries to fill that void by living vicariously through the children. In doing so, however, a measure of their identity becomes bound up in them. Consequently, when the kids leave, a part of the parent leaves with them, and the withdrawal pains can be excruciating.

Sometimes the Parental Relationship Overshadows the Marital Relationship

Another cause for difficulty in releasing children can be deduced from Ephesians 5:22–33. In this text, God discusses the home with husbands and wives.

> Wives, be subject to your own husbands. . . .
> Husbands, love your wives. . . . Husbands ought
> also to love their own wives as their own bodies.
> . . . Nevertheless let each individual among you
> also love his own wife even as himself; and let the
> wife see to it that she respect her husband.

Did you notice who's conspicuously missing in this passage? Children. Why? Because the basic relationship in the home is *not* the parent-child relationship, but the husband-wife relationship. Children were never designed to be the weld that holds a family together.

For many husbands and wives, however, releasing the children is extremely difficult because the parental relationship has become stronger than the marriage relationship. Insecure parents, who have gathered emotional strength from their children that they should have found in their mate, cannot cope with this release phase. As the children cut their ties to the home and move out on their own, the single thread that tied the parents to personal fulfillment is also cut. The release becomes a time of mourning and depression that often leads to divorce.

Husbands and wives, are you establishing a relationship that revolves around your children or around each other? If it is centered on your children, time will disintegrate that core, and your marriage will collapse in the vacuum of their absence.

Sometimes Parents Possess a Consuming Need for Their Children

Still another obstacle making release difficult can be drawn from 2 Corinthians 12. Speaking as a father to his child, the apostle Paul announces his plans to visit the church he founded in Corinth.

> Here for this third time I am ready to come to you, and I will not be a burden to you; for I do not seek what is yours, but you; for children are not responsible to save up for their parents, but parents for their children. (v. 14)

In a tactful way, Paul is saying that he is not coming for money but for them. As their spiritual father, he wants to serve them, not have them serve him. To underscore his purpose, he uses the maxim that children do not support the parents, but parents support the children. It is the basic responsibility of the mother and father to provide for the needs of the children, not the other way around.

An important application for us to remember is that parents should not have children because they *need* them, but because they *want* them. Children should be a by-product of love between a husband and wife, not a desperate attempt to create a support system for either spouse. Parents who possess an unhealthy need to be supported by their children, as opposed to a healthy desire to support them, will resist releasing them completely.

How to Prepare for Releasing Your Child

Assuming that you let your children have their own identity, that you don't depend on them to hold your marriage together, and that you are supporting them instead of the other way around, letting go may still be difficult—but not devastating. Turning now from the problems to the solutions, how should we prepare for the time of release? Here are four important insights—two negative, two positive—to consider.

First: Children Should Not Be Handed Life on a Silver Platter

We need to *train* our children to handle our legacy, not just hand it over to them. For a closer look at what we mean, consider the following words, spoken by an embittered man looking at life strictly from an earthly point of view.

> Thus I hated all the fruit of my labor for which I had labored under the sun, for I must leave it to the man who will come after me. And who knows whether he will be a wise man or a fool? Yet he will have control over all the fruit of my labor for which I have labored by acting wisely under the sun. This too is vanity. Therefore I completely despaired of all the fruit of my labor for which I had labored under the sun. (Eccles. 2:18–20)

The father described in this passage had worked hard to make his business a success—hammering away, building, and fine-tuning. Long hours were invested and the pressure was high, but he finally got the business off the ground. Once airborne, it soared; but then so did the father's blood pressure. Chest pains began to worsen, and he had to bail out. He turned to his copilot son, who had been allowed to sightsee but was never taught to fly. With naive eagerness and a newfound sense of power, the son grabbed the controls and said, "No problem, Dad." But before the joyride had barely begun, the business went into a tailspin, and—CRASH!

The team sent to investigate the wreckage unanimously concluded the crash was caused by pilot error. The son had never learned the disciplines involved in getting a business off the ground and keeping it in the air. Looking mournfully at the crash site, the investigators mumbled to themselves some belated wisdom from the Scriptures. Under the breath of one was heard,

> "If you have run with footmen and they have
>   tired you out,
> Then how can you compete with the horses?
> If you fall down in a land of peace,
> How will you do in the thicket of the Jordan?"
> (Jer. 12:5)

If your children can't cut it at home in such things as cleaning up their rooms, making their beds, and carrying out other minor responsibilities, what on earth will they do when they face the horses of a competitive career or the thicket of marital adjustments? Another investigator muttered as he walked away,

> It is good for a man that he should bear
> The yoke in his youth. (Lam. 3:27)

Hard work, sacrifice, and responsibility appropriate to their ages are healthy yokes for young people to shoulder. They will be stretched and strengthened in preparation for the years to come. Are you preparing your children for the yoke of adult life—or are you preparing them for disaster by pampering them?

Second: Don't Stop Communicating with Your Children after They Leave

Remember, releasing your children doesn't mean you should never again offer advice or encouragement. On the contrary, a parent's counsel can continue to be of great value to a child after he or she has left home. "Leaving father and mother" doesn't mean children are to leave them out of their lives. Proverbs 23:22 strikes an encouraging balance:

> Listen to your father who begot you,
> And do not despise your mother when she is old.

A word of caution, however, is in order for the parents. Once your children leave the nest, your relationship with them changes. Now they must make their own decisions, run their own lives. If asked, or when appropriate, give them counsel[1]—but let them exercise the important right of making their own decisions. They must, if they're to mature to be strong on their own.

Third: Look upon Release as a Process Rather Than a Sudden Event

Psalm 144:12 somewhat captures this process of preparation.

> Let our sons in their youth be as grown-up plants,
> And our daughters as corner pillars fashioned as for
> a palace.

---

1. The book of Proverbs is a gold mine of wisdom regarding the right use of words. They should be words that express wisdom (15:2a), that are carefully chosen (15:28a), that are fitting to the circumstance (25:11), timely (15:23), pleasant and refreshing (16:24), and finally, that are few (10:19).

This is a picture of careful nurturing and skillful planning with regard to the process of raising children. A by-product of preparing children for the seasons and weight of adult life is that the parents themselves become prepared for their release in the process.

Fourth: Commit Yourself to Pray for Your Children

Commit yourself to a ministry of continued prayer for your children. Susanna Wesley is a memorable example of this. Altogether, she bore nineteen children. Several died as infants, but those who lived were more than a houseful. Despite the incredible demands put upon her as a mother, Mrs. Wesley gave an hour a week to each child while they were in the home. Still more amazing, when a child left home, she invested that same hour during the week in prayer for that son or daughter.

Job was also committed to praying for his children (Job 1:4–5). Are you praying regularly, earnestly for your children? Pray for them while they're at home; sharpen and straighten the arrows; and when you finally release them—pray they're on target and that they don't fall short of the glory of God.

Conclusion

As a final reminder, let's review the four essential insights for releasing our children by drawing some spiritual analogies. First, God does not give His children life on a silver platter. Jesus doesn't offer protection from troubles in this life; rather, He provides us with the strength and the grace to glorify Him in our response to them. Growth and maturity aren't handed out indiscriminately as treats, they are earned through tough trials and unflagging endurance.

Second, God does not stop communicating with His children the more mature they become. Quite the opposite. The more we abide in Him, the more we see and know of Him.

Third, God looks upon releasing as a process. Little by little He entrusts us with more and more responsibility. We learn to crawl, then He teaches us to walk. We learn to walk, then He teaches us to run. At every stage He stretches our spiritual muscles to develop them to their full potential.

Finally, God's Son, Jesus Christ, intercedes for us before the Father's throne (see Heb. 7:25). The firstborn of all creation never forgets, never tires, never gets distracted in his vigil to pray on our behalf.

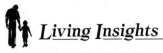# Living Insights

Mom and Dad, do you want to know how to cripple your children so that they can never leave the home? Do you want to know how to make them fear adulthood, fear being on their own, paralyze them for life so that they become dependent upon you permanently?

- Ignore their feelings and wishes.

- Tell them what they feel and want.

- Make all their decisions for them.

Do that consistently and you'll break every independent bone in your son's or daughter's body. They'll never be able to mentally leave your home and establish one of their own.

How many of you adults reading this Living Insight are still dependent on your moms or dads to make decisions for you? How many of you, looking back at the difficult decisions you faced this past year, find that you let your parents or a parent figure decide for you because you were too scared to decide for yourself?

Why are we scared? For many it's because our parents never released to us the responsibility of decision making so that we could learn how to do it ourselves. We've been conditioned not to decide but to let someone else decide for us. That sabotages our growth, our maturity, and our future.

Mom and Dad, release to your children the appropriate freedom as well as the responsibility to make choices and shoulder consequences. Let them learn how to make decisions; teach them how to discern good from evil; how to weigh the pros and cons and make informed, intelligent choices. Only by practice and guided trial and error will your children gain the confidence and skill they will need as adults.

What kind of children are you trying to raise and release? Mature, independent, godly kids—or dependent, emotional cripples who must struggle through adulthood as perpetual adolescents? You decide.[2]

2. For further in-depth study concerning this, read Jerry and Mary White's book *When Your Kids Aren't Kids Anymore* (Colorado Springs, Colo.: NavPress, 1989); and chapter 14, "Teaching Children to Be Responsible," in *Dr. Dobson Answers Your Questions* (Wheaton, Ill.: Tyndale House Publishers, 1982).

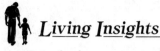 *Living Insights*

Your final assignment in this study on parenting is to go back over each of the chapters listed and record the insights that have been most meaningful and helpful to you. Let this be a way of summarizing the truths you want to apply in your home.

1. Knowing Your Child _____

_____

2. Breaking Granddad's Bent _____

_____

3. Loving Your Child _____

_____

4. You Can't Have One without the Other _____

_____

5. Shaping the Will with Wisdom _____

_____

6. The Ministry of the Rod _____

_____

7. Training Your Child _____

_____

8. The Home Training of Jesus _____

_____

9. Seeds a Mother Plants _____

_____

10. Masculine Model of Leadership _____

Congratulations on completing this course on parenting! As a graduation gift to yourself, we want you to do something that all parents forget to do at times—play. You'll feel better after you do, and your children will certainly benefit from your having rested and relaxed.

If money is tight, ask a friend to keep your kids for the weekend and just stay home. Then sleep in, drink a cup of coffee, drink two, read the newspaper without any interruptions, play tennis, see a movie, read a book, talk, dance, eat out, ride a bike, take a luxurious bath, do whatever it is you want to do for a change. Treat yourself! You'll love it, and we think you deserve it.

BOOKS FOR
PROBING FURTHER

People often talk about the miracle of birth, but what about the miracle of successfully training up children in the way they should go?

Anybody who's been through parenthood can tell you that that's no small miracle either. Helping children in their protracted struggle to emerge from the family womb as whole, healthy, godly individuals is an incredible task. And the smoothness of the delivery in this interpersonal miracle depends a great deal on the parents.

Are you well prepared? Will your love and leadership provide a safe haven in which your children can develop? Will they feel secure, be protected, and have the spiritual and emotional nourishment needed to grow and mature?

None of us will ever feel completely adequate for the task. It's as if God has given parents the responsibility for something we know is beyond our powers to accomplish. That's why it is so important to study His Word and seek His help in training our children. He has written the manual on this miracle, and we're to meditate on it day and night so we "may be careful to do according to all that is written in it" (Josh. 1:8).

For those of you wanting to dig deeper and receive more training from the Scriptures as well as from other godly men and women, here are some excellent resources.

General Study

Blue, Ron and Judy. *Money Matters for Parents and Their Kids*. Nashville, Tenn.: Thomas Nelson Publishers, Oliver-Nelson Books, 1988.

Curran, Dolores. *Traits of a Healthy Family*. San Francisco, Calif.: Harper and Row, Publishers, 1983.

Dobson, James. *Dr. Dobson Answers Your Questions*. Wheaton, Ill.: Tyndale House Publishers, 1982.

———. *Hide or Seek*. Revised edition. Old Tappan, N.J.: Fleming H. Revell Co., 1979.

Lindskoog, John and Kathryn. *How to Grow a Young Reader.* Wheaton, Ill.: Harold Shaw Publishers, 1989.

Smalley, Gary. *The Key to Your Child's Heart.* Dallas, Tex.: Word Publishing, 1984.

Swindoll, Charles R. *You and Your Child.* Nashville, Tenn.: Thomas Nelson Publishers, 1977.

Moms and Dads

Canfield, Ken R. *The Seven Secrets of Effective Fathers.* Wheaton, Ill.: Tyndale House Publishers, 1992.

Peel, Kathy and Joy Mahaffey. *A Mother's Manual for Summer Survival.* Pomona, Calif.: Focus on the Family Publishing, 1989.

Rushford, Patricia H. *What Kids Need Most in a Mom.* Old Tappan, N.J.: Fleming H. Revell Co., 1989.

Parents with Special Needs

Aldrich, Sandra Picklesimer. *From One Single Mother to Another.* Ventura, Calif.: Gospel Light Publications, Regal Books, 1991.

Barnes, Robert. *You're Not My Daddy: The Step-Parenting Process.* Dallas, Tex.: Word Publishing, 1992.

Dobson, James. "Mothers of Handicapped Children." Audiocassette tape. Available through Focus on the Family, Colorado Springs, Colorado 80995.

Frydenger, Tom and Adrienne. *The Blended Family.* Tarrytown, N.Y.: Fleming H. Revell Co., Chosen Books, 1984.

Lewis, Derek, Nancy, and Michael, and James Dobson. "Raising a Handicapped Child." Audiocassette tape. Available through Focus on the Family, Colorado Springs, Colorado 80995.

Richmond, Gary. *Successful Single Parenting.* Eugene, Oreg.: Harvest House Publishers, 1990.

Roberts, Nancy. *Help for the Parents of a Handicapped Child.* St. Louis, Mo.: Concordia Publishing House, 1981.

Wheeler, Bonnie. *Challenged Parenting: A Practical Handbook for Parents of Children with Handicaps.* Ventura, Calif.: Gospel Light

Publications, Regal Books, 1982.

For Your Child's Spiritual Growth

Lewis, Paul. *Forty Ways to Teach Your Child Values*. Wheaton, Ill.: Tyndale House Publishers, Living Books, 1985.

Williford, Carolyn. *Devotions for Families That Can't Sit Still*. Wheaton, Ill.: Scripture Press Publications, Victor Books, 1990.

Disciplining Your Child

Dobson, James. *The New Dare to Discipline*. Wheaton, Ill.: Tyndale House Publishers, 1992. Completely revised edition of Dobson's 1970 best-seller, *Dare to Discipline*.

Ray, Bruce A. *Withhold Not Correction*. Phillipsburg, N.J.: Presbyterian and Reformed Publishing Co., 1978.

Building Memories

Gaither, Gloria and Shirley Dobson. *Let's Make a Memory*. Dallas, Tex.: Word Books, 1983.

Gire, Ken. *The Gift of Remembrance*. Grand Rapids, Mich.: Zondervan Publishing House, Daybreak Books, 1990. This has since been retitled *A Father's Gift* by Zondervan.

Great Reading for Children

Focus on the Family. This ministry has four great magazines for children: *Clubhouse Jr.*, ages four to eight; *Clubhouse*, ages eight to twelve; *Breakaway*, for guys twelve and up; and *Brio*, for girls twelve and up. They are available through Focus on the Family, Colorado Springs, Colorado 80995.

Gire, Judy. *A Boy and His Baseball: The Dave Dravecky Story*. Grand Rapids, Mich.: Zondervan Publishing House, 1992. For ages four through ten.

Gire, Ken. *Adventures in the Big Thicket*. Pomona, Calif.: Focus on the Family Publishers, 1990. All ages.

———. *Treasure in an Oatmeal Box*. Colorado Springs, Colo.: NavPress, 1990. For ages nine through twelve. Gold Medallion winner.

Henley, Karyn. *The Beginner's Bible: Timeless Children's Stories.* Sisters, Oreg.: Questar Publishers, 1989. For preschoolers.

Lewis, C. S. *The Chronicles of Narnia.* Seven volumes. New York, N.Y.: Macmillan Publishing Co., 1950–56. These classic tales will appeal to nine-year-olds through adults.

Lindvall, Ella K. *Read-Aloud Bible Stories.* Three volumes. Chicago, Ill.: Moody Press, 1982, 1985, 1990. Volume 1 was a Gold Medallion winner.

Paterson, Katherine. *Bridge to Terabithia.* New York, N.Y.: Thomas Y. Crowell Co., 1977.

Spier, Peter. *Noah's Ark.* New York, N.Y.: Doubleday, 1977. For preschoolers.

Wilde, Oscar. *The Happy Prince.* Available through a number of publishers. For ages seven through ten.

————. *The Selfish Giant.* Available through a number of publishers. For ages six through ten.

Some of the books listed here may be out of print and available only through a library. All of these works are recommended reading only. With the exception of books by Charles R. Swindoll, none of them are available through Insight for Living. If you wish to obtain some of these suggested readings, please contact your local Christian bookstore.

NOTES

NOTES

NOTES

NOTES

ORDERING INFORMATION

Cassette Tapes and Study Guide

This Bible study guide was designed to be used independently or in conjunction with the broadcast of Chuck Swindoll's taped messages on the topic listed below. If you would like to order cassette tapes or further copies of this study guide, please see the information given below and the Order Forms provided at the end of this guide.

YOU AND YOUR CHILD

No other job on earth is more complicated, more demanding, or more time-consuming than that of rearing a child. Yet many parents take on this high calling with less formal training than they received while learning their ABCs. And it shows. Look around—the hurt, pain, and frustration in homes today is at an all-time high.

Thankfully, we have a heavenly Father who has provided us with the basic training we need. The Bible doesn't simply offer theories, it gives us truth—solid, dependable, workable principles for accomplishing the incredible task of rearing godly children.

Open your Bible and join us as we examine God's curriculum concerning you and your child. Study His methods, practice His precepts, and you'll find that no other job can be more rewarding, bring more joy, or result in more satisfaction than being a parent.

		Calif.*	U.S.	B.C.*	Canada*
YYC CS	Cassette series, includes album cover	$52.39	$48.85	$62.00	$58.00
YYC 1–7	Individual cassettes, includes messages A and B	6.76	6.30	8.90	8.50
YYC SG	Study guide	5.31	4.95	6.50	6.50

*These prices already include the following charges: for delivery in **California**, applicable sales tax; **Canada**, 7% GST and 7% postage and handling (on tapes only); **British Columbia**, 7% GST, 6% British Columbia sales tax (on tapes only), and 7% postage and handling (on tapes only). **The prices are subject to change without notice.**

YYC 1-A: *Knowing Your Child*—Proverbs 22:6; Psalm 139:13–16
      B: *Breaking Granddad's Bent*—Exodus 34:5–8; Selected Scriptures

YYC 2-A: *Loving Your Child*—Psalms 127:1–128:3
      B: *You Can't Have One without the Other*—Genesis 25–28

YYC 3-A: *Shaping the Will with Wisdom*—Selected Proverbs
     B: *The Ministry of the Rod*—1 Samuel 2:12–3:13

YYC 4-A: *Training Your Child*—Deuteronomy 6:1–9
     B: *The Home Training of Jesus*—Luke 2:39–52

YYC 5-A: *Seeds a Mother Plants*—2 Timothy 1:1–7
     B: *Masculine Model of Leadership*—Selected Scriptures

YYC 6-A: *You and Your Daughter (Part One)*—Selected Proverbs
     B: *You and Your Daughter (Part Two)*—Selected Proverbs

YYC 7-A: *You and Your Son*—Selected Proverbs
     B: *Releasing Your Child*—Selected Scriptures

How to Order by Mail

Simply mark on the order form whether you want the series or individual tapes. Mail the form with your payment to the appropriate address listed below. We will process your order as promptly as we can.

United States: Mail your order to the Ordering Services Department at Insight for Living, Post Office Box 69000, Anaheim, California 92817-0900. If you wish your order to be shipped first-class for faster delivery, add 10 percent of the total order amount. Otherwise, please allow four to six weeks for delivery by fourth-class mail. We accept payment by personal check, money order, or credit card. Unfortunately, we are unable to offer invoicing or COD orders.

Canada: Mail your order to Insight for Living Ministries, Post Office Box 2510, Vancouver, British Columbia V6B 3W7. Allow approximately four weeks for delivery. We accept payment by personal check, money order, or credit card. Unfortunately, we are unable to offer invoicing or COD orders.

Australia, New Zealand, or Papua New Guinea: Mail your order to Insight for Living, Inc., GPO Box 2823 EE, Melbourne, Victoria 3001, Australia. Please allow six to ten weeks for delivery by surface mail. If you would like your order sent airmail, the delivery time may be reduced. Using the United States price as a base, add postage costs—surface or airmail—to the amount of your order. Please use the chart that follows to determine correct postage. Due to fluctuating currency rates, we can accept only personal checks made payable in United States funds, international money orders, or credit cards in payment for materials.

Overseas: Other overseas residents should mail their orders to our United States office. Please allow six to ten weeks for delivery by surface mail. If you would like your order sent airmail, the delivery time may be reduced. Using the United States price as a base, add postage costs— surface or airmail—to the amount of your order. Please use the chart that follows to determine correct postage. Due to fluctuating currency rates, we can accept only personal checks made payable in United States funds, international money orders, or credit cards in payment for materials.

Type of Postage	Postage Cost
Surface	10% of total order
Airmail	25% of total order

For Faster Service, Order by Telephone or FAX

For credit card orders, you are welcome to use one of our toll-free numbers between the hours of 7:00 A.M. and 4:30 P.M., Pacific time, Monday through Friday, or our FAX numbers. The numbers to use from anywhere in the United States are **1-800-772-8888** or FAX (714) 575-5496. To order from Canada, call our Vancouver office using **1-800-663-7639** or FAX (604) 596-2975. Vancouver residents, call (604) 596-2910. Australian residents should phone (03) 872-4606. From other international locations, call our Ordering Services Department at (714) 575-5000 in the United States.

Our Guarantee

Our cassettes are guaranteed for ninety days against faulty performance or breakage due to a defect in the tape. For best results, please be sure your tape recorder is in good operating condition and is cleaned regularly.

Note: To cover processing and handling, there is a $10 fee for *any* returned check.

Insight for Living Catalog

Request a free copy of the Insight for Living catalog of books, tapes, and study guides by calling **1-800-772-8888** in the United States or **1-800-663-7639** in Canada.

Order Form

YYC CS represents the entire *You and Your Child* series in a special album cover, while YYC 1–7 are the individual tapes included in the series. YYC SG represents this study guide, should you desire to order additional copies.

Item	Calif.*	Unit Price U.S.	B.C.*	Canada*	Quantity	Amount
YYC CS	$52.39	$48.85	$62.00	$58.00		$
YYC 1	6.76	6.30	8.90	8.50		
YYC 2	6.76	6.30	8.90	8.50		
YYC 3	6.76	6.30	8.90	8.50		
YYC 4	6.76	6.30	8.90	8.50		
YYC 5	6.76	6.30	8.90	8.50		
YYC 6	6.76	6.30	8.90	8.50		
YYC 7	6.76	6.30	8.90	8.50		
YYC SG	5.31	4.95	6.50	6.50		
					Subtotal	
		Overseas Residents *Pay U.S. price plus 10% surface postage or 25% airmail. Also, see "How to Order by Mail."*				
		U.S. First-Class Shipping *For faster delivery, add 10% for postage and handling.*				
		Gift to Insight for Living *Tax-deductible in the United States and Canada.*				
		Total Amount Due *Please do not send cash.*				$

If there is a balance: ❑ Apply it as a donation ❑ Please refund
*These prices already include applicable taxes and shipping costs.

Payment by: ❑ Check or money order payable to Insight for Living ❑ Credit card

(Circle one): Visa MasterCard Discover Card Number _____

Expiration Date _____ Signature _____
                                   We cannot process your credit card purchase without your signature.

Name _____

Address _____

City _____ State/Province _____

Zip/Postal Code _____ Country _____

Telephone (___) _____ Radio Station ____ ____ ____ ____
If questions arise concerning your order, we may need to contact you.

Mail this order form to the Ordering Services Department at one of these addresses:
Insight for Living, Post Office Box 69000, Anaheim, CA 92817-0900
Insight for Living Ministries, Post Office Box 2510, Vancouver, BC, Canada V6B 3W7
Insight for Living, Inc., GPO Box 2823 EE, Melbourne, VIC 3001, Australia

Order Form

YYC CS represents the entire *You and Your Child* series in a special album cover, while YYC 1–7 are the individual tapes included in the series. YYC SG represents this study guide, should you desire to order additional copies.

Item	Calif.*	Unit Price U.S.	B.C.*	Canada*	Quantity	Amount
YYC CS	$52.39	$48.85	$62.00	$58.00		$
YYC 1	6.76	6.30	8.90	8.50		
YYC 2	6.76	6.30	8.90	8.50		
YYC 3	6.76	6.30	8.90	8.50		
YYC 4	6.76	6.30	8.90	8.50		
YYC 5	6.76	6.30	8.90	8.50		
YYC 6	6.76	6.30	8.90	8.50		
YYC 7	6.76	6.30	8.90	8.50		
YYC SG	5.31	4.95	6.50	6.50		
					Subtotal	
					Overseas Residents *Pay U.S. price plus 10% surface postage or 25% airmail. Also, see "How to Order by Mail."*	
					U.S. First-Class Shipping *For faster delivery, add 10% for postage and handling.*	
					Gift to Insight for Living *Tax-deductible in the United States and Canada.*	
					Total Amount Due *Please do not send cash.*	$

If there is a balance: ❏ Apply it as a donation ❏ Please refund
*These prices already include applicable taxes and shipping costs.

Payment by: ❏ Check or money order payable to Insight for Living ❏ Credit card

(Circle one): Visa MasterCard Discover Card Number＿＿＿＿＿＿＿＿＿

Expiration Date＿＿＿＿＿ Signature＿＿＿＿＿＿＿＿＿＿＿＿＿＿＿
We cannot process your credit card purchase without your signature.

Name＿＿＿＿＿＿＿＿＿＿＿＿＿＿＿＿＿＿＿＿＿＿＿＿＿＿＿

Address＿＿＿＿＿＿＿＿＿＿＿＿＿＿＿＿＿＿＿＿＿＿＿＿＿

City＿＿＿＿＿＿＿＿＿＿＿＿＿＿＿ State/Province＿＿＿＿＿

Zip/Postal Code＿＿＿＿＿＿＿ Country＿＿＿＿＿＿＿＿＿

Telephone (＿＿) ＿＿＿＿＿＿＿ Radio Station＿＿ ＿＿ ＿＿ ＿＿
If questions arise concerning your order, we may need to contact you.

Mail this order form to the Ordering Services Department at one of these addresses:
Insight for Living, Post Office Box 69000, Anaheim, CA 92817-0900
Insight for Living Ministries, Post Office Box 2510, Vancouver, BC, Canada V6B 3W7
Insight for Living, Inc., GPO Box 2823 EE, Melbourne, VIC 3001, Australia

Order Form

YYC CS represents the entire *You and Your Child* series in a special album cover, while YYC 1–7 are the individual tapes included in the series. YYC SG represents this study guide, should you desire to order additional copies.

Item	Calif.*	Unit Price U.S.	B.C.*	Canada*	Quantity	Amount
YYC CS	$52.39	$48.85	$62.00	$58.00		$
YYC 1	6.76	6.30	8.90	8.50		
YYC 2	6.76	6.30	8.90	8.50		
YYC 3	6.76	6.30	8.90	8.50		
YYC 4	6.76	6.30	8.90	8.50		
YYC 5	6.76	6.30	8.90	8.50		
YYC 6	6.76	6.30	8.90	8.50		
YYC 7	6.76	6.30	8.90	8.50		
YYC SG	5.31	4.95	6.50	6.50		
					Subtotal	
		Overseas Residents Pay U.S. price plus 10% surface postage or 25% airmail. Also, see "How to Order by Mail."				
		U.S. First-Class Shipping For faster delivery, add 10% for postage and handling.				
		Gift to Insight for Living Tax-deductible in the United States and Canada.				
		Total Amount Due Please do not send cash.				$

If there is a balance: ❏ Apply it as a donation ❏ Please refund
*These prices already include applicable taxes and shipping costs.

Payment by: ❏ Check or money order payable to Insight for Living ❏ Credit card

(Circle one): Visa   MasterCard   Discover Card   Number _____

Expiration Date _____   Signature _____
We cannot process your credit card purchase without your signature.

Name _____

Address _____

City _____ State/Province _____

Zip/Postal Code _____ Country _____

Telephone ( ) _____ Radio Station ____ ____ ____ ____
If questions arise concerning your order, we may need to contact you.

Mail this order form to the Ordering Services Department at one of these addresses:
Insight for Living, Post Office Box 69000, Anaheim, CA 92817-0900
Insight for Living Ministries, Post Office Box 2510, Vancouver, BC, Canada V6B 3W7
Insight for Living, Inc., GPO Box 2823 EE, Melbourne, VIC 3001, Australia